"God has a blueprint, us must be seen through the le ... I know of no better guide than Pu ...ke you on a journey of discovering how your li an have a Kingdom impact that will touch and transform the world in you and around you. *Kingdom Impact* is a must-read for those who are desiring to reclaim God's original purposes for their lives."

Leif Hetland, president and founder, Global Mission Awareness; author, *Called to Reign* and *Giant Slayers*

"Dr. Putty Putman is a brilliant yet humble man. *Kingdom Impact* is one of the most interesting and exciting books that I have read in a while. It is theological, practical and personal. I believe anyone who wants to have a biblical basis for understanding the power of the Holy Spirit and His gifts, and a practical understanding of how to partner with God, will want to read *Kingdom Impact*."

Dr. Randy Clark, overseer, Apostolic Network of Global Awakening; president, Global Awakening Theological Seminary

"In *Kingdom Impact*, Putty brings fresh revelation and keen insight concerning our destiny as children of the King. He speaks powerfully and prophetically about the historical time we are in and the incredible privilege we have of partnering with the Spirit to make Kingdom impact. As his pastor, I weekly get to watch him live what he so brilliantly writes!"

Happy and Dianne Leman, founding pastors, The Vineyard Church of Central Illinois

"Our world is at war, and God's will doesn't enter the world uncontested. In *Kingdom Impact*, Putty has given you the keys you need to reclaim your world, and our whole world, through the power of the Holy Spirit. Don't waste another day without partnering with Him!"

Laura Harris Smith, C.N.C., M.S.O.M., author, *The Healthy Living Handbook* and *Get Well Soon*; host, *theTHREE*

"First John 4:4 (KJV) says, 'Greater is he that is in you, than he that is in the world.' The word *you* in that verse is plural. *Kingdom Impact* awakens readers to this overlooked truth: The Kingdom, empowered by the Spirit, is a collective force guided intelligently by God's unseen hand."

Dr. Michael S. Heiser, scholar-in-residence, Faithlife / Logos
Bible Software; author, *The Unseen Realm*;
host, *The Naked Bible Podcast*

"In the pages of this masterful work, Dr. Putty Putman unpacks the power, purpose and impact of the Kingdom of God for everyday believers. If you want to learn what Jesus meant when He said 'on earth as it is in Heaven' and how to walk in the supernatural daily, this is for you. I encourage every person to read and carefully consider the revelation in this work, which will prepare you for real-life Kingdom ministry."

Dr. Kynan Bridges, author, *90 Days of Power Prayer*;
senior pastor, Grace & Peace Global Fellowship, Inc.

"Throughout my ministerial career, there are a few teachings I have heard that stand out over the rest. One of them is Putty's teaching on the reformation at hand and the role of 'interdependence' in the middle of what the Father is doing. In this book, you will see what it looks like for all of God's kids to play a role in His work. We must all take seriously what our roles are in advancing God's Kingdom, and in this new book from Putty, he will challenge you to do so through humility, clarity and invitation. I love Putty as an author, pastor and friend. The church I pastor is still talking about the impact that this content is having on them. You will thoroughly enjoy being impacted by the gift on Putty's life."

Chad Norris, lead pastor, Bridgeway Church; author, *Mama
Jane's Secret: Walking in Deep Friendship with God*

KINGDOM IMPACT

KINGDOM IMPACT

LIVING LIKE JESUS IN A BROKEN WORLD

PUTTY PUTMAN

Chosen

a division of Baker Publishing Group
Minneapolis, Minnesota

Published by Chosen Books
11400 Hampshire Avenue South
Bloomington, Minnesota 55438
www.chosenbooks.com

Chosen Books is a division of
Baker Publishing Group, Grand Rapids, Michigan

Printed in the United States of America

Library of Congress Cataloging-in-Publication Data
Names: Putman, Putty, author.
Title: Kingdom impact : living like Jesus in a broken world / Putty Putman.
Description: Minneapolis : Chosen, a division of Baker Publishing Group, 2019.
 | Includes bibliographical references.
Identifiers: LCCN 2018042372 | ISBN 9780800798536 (pbk.) | ISBN
 9781493417353 (e-book)
Subjects: LCSH: Christian life. | Kingdom of God. | Jesus Christ—Kingdom. |
 Jesus Christ–Example.
Classification: LCC BV4501.3 .P885 2019 | DDC 248.4—dc23
LC record available at https://lccn.loc.gov/2018042372

Cover design by Studio Gearbox

19 20 21 22 23 24 25   7 6 5 4 3 2 1

To the Holy Spirit—the One who brings God's inbreaking Kingdom. And to the Vineyard Church of Central Illinois. Without you, I never would have stumbled onto "the pearl of great price."

CONTENTS

FOREWORD

PUTTY PUTMAN is a revivalist, Kingdom equipper and man of God who has been called for such a time as this. He is uniquely gifted to raise up reformers who walk in signs and wonders. Putty has given birth to a book that is more than mere words; it is a prophetic mandate for what God is doing on the earth at this moment in history.

Kingdom Impact will inspire you to leave the safety of predictable living and launch out into the treacherous waters of a supernatural life. This book reminds me of the Lord's Prayer that Jesus taught His disciples in the midst of the darkest season in human history. In the depths of Roman oppression, with the reign of the evil emperor Nero within a stone's throw of history, Jesus turned to His disciples and said, "Pray that My Father's Kingdom will come and that His will be done on earth, as it is in heaven." This prayer is at the very heart of Putty's book! That's why I believe *Kingdom Impact* will be a catalyst of cultural transformation by fueling a dramatic paradigm shift in the Church.

This book will transform everyday people such as doctors, housewives, mechanics, computer programmers, schoolteachers and business managers and equip them to destroy the works of the devil as they demonstrate the power of the superior Kingdom everywhere they go!

Kingdom Impact is a timely, practical and God-inspired message as Jesus calls His Church to revival and reformation. I have no doubt that you will find inspiration in Putty's words to take up your responsibility as an heir to God's throne and begin bringing the Kingdom with confidence and God's undeniable power. May it be in your life as it is in heaven, and may God's Kingdom come, until our world looks like His world.

Kris Vallotton, leader, Bethel Church, Redding, California;
co-founder, Bethel School of Supernatural Ministry;
author of thirteen books, including *The Supernatural Ways of Royalty, Heavy Rain* and *Poverty, Riches and Wealth*

ACKNOWLEDGMENTS

THE JOURNEY of writing a book is a long one, and credit is due to far more than just the person who winds up with his or her name on the cover.

My nuclear family deserves quite a bit of credit. In the midst of far too much to do and Dad increasingly zigzagging across the world, you have sacrificed even more time to allow me to pursue this project. Thank you for sharing me with these readers. I love the life we are all building together.

I owe my parents a great debt of gratitude as well, especially my dad, who has always carried a passion for writing. Thanks for instilling in me a belief that I should pursue my passions and experience the joy of creating.

To my family at the Vineyard Church of Central Illinois: We are on such a thrilling adventure. Thank you for being willing to pursue God in every way. I think it is so special that in us God has found a family willing to strike out and see the unknown in Him.

Hap and Di: It goes without saying that none of this would be here without you both, but I am going to say it anyway. Thank you a hundred times over for seeing what God has put in me and for opening doors for me to walk through. If, in any way, I see further than some others, it is because I stand on the shoulders of giants.

Mike, Julie, Jim: I cannot imagine a better team with whom to chase after God's dreams for the Church. The first forty years have been incredible, but I have a hunch the best is yet ahead.

"ARC" team: Thank you for being willing to dream larger than most people will let themselves imagine. I truly believe the stuff we turn over is someday going to wind up in history books. Thank you for all your sacrifice, your incredible hard work and your perseverance for the vision.

To everyone from every church who is on this journey with us: Let us keep pressing forward. A new chapter in the Church does not come easily, but it is what is needed in our day. Why not us? Why not now? We can do what God has set upon our hearts.

To Chosen Books: Thank you again for a wonderful experience putting this book together. I have enjoyed both of these projects more than I anticipated. You are a blast to work with, and you bring an excellence that pushes my writing to the next level. Thank you for empowering this journey.

There are doubtless many more I am sure I have forgotten to express my gratitude to, and for that I apologize. Thank you to each and every person who has been a part of this journey and who has held me up one way or another. I could not have done it without you.

AN UNLIKELY INTRODUCTION

CONFUSED AND FLUSTERED, I made my way to the center of the room. We were in a hotel suite in China, holding an illegal meeting with about a dozen house church leaders of the underground Chinese Christian Church. The whole experience was surreal; we had to keep a low profile on our way in and out, staying quiet so as not to attract attention.

Our goal that day was to train these church leaders with a simple prayer model to get them started praying for the sick. The only catch was, I did not pray for the sick. I did not even really believe in this whole thing. I had grown up as a Bible-centered evangelical Baptist. Jesus I knew; He was familiar, and I did what I could to follow the life He portrayed, but edgy things like praying for healing or prophesying? Count me out.

How did this happen? I don't do this stuff; I don't even really believe in this stuff. Despite my confusion and doubt, the leaders looked at me expectantly, anticipating that the American missionary would put all this into practice like a pro.

My mind raced as I tried to find a path forward. *Come on, Putty. You have no idea what you're doing, but they don't know that. Just repeat what you saw in that class a few weeks back and it'll be good enough. The team leader who is translating can fix any major mistakes.*

I asked the woman standing in the center of the prayer circle with me a few simple questions about how long ago her wrist had been injured and if she minded if I put my hand on her shoulder while we prayed. She indicated that it was all right, so, placing my hand on her shoulder, I repeated verbatim what I had heard the trainer say in my class. "We invite the Holy Spirit because He is the one who has healing, not us." Skeptical as I had been while sitting in the training class, this prayer apparently stuck.

Then I prayed the prayer that changed everything in my life: "Come, Holy Spirit."

Some Background

I grew up in the Christian faith, receiving what I perceive to be a rather typical evangelical church upbringing. I was actively involved in the local church from a very young age, and my faith has been central to my life since I was a child. My church experience centered on the Scriptures and sound teaching. I acquired a deep value for the Bible and aimed to live my life according to its teachings.

Through junior high and high school, I became more and more involved in the church, voluntarily leading in our youth group and participating on our worship team (mostly because of need, not because of my ability). By the time I was ready for college, I decided to go to a Christian school—Bethel University (at the time Bethel College) in St. Paul, Minnesota. There, my faith continued to grow in depth and understanding. I majored in physics, but I took a standard set of courses on Church history, Christian theology and the like.

did just that. I would not have found myself in that hotel room in China without God keeping me in the dark about what He was really up to.

In the four years that we attended the Vineyard church, Brittany and I became involved with the international ministry at our church. This seemed a natural fit for me. When I was about seven years old, my parents moved to mainland China to be missionaries for a year. Dad taught English at a university, and Mom was home with my brother and me. They both discipled people as opportunities presented themselves.

As a seven-year-old, seeing this process up close was significant for me. First, it made me take faith seriously. Seeing people risk jail to be discipled in following Jesus proved there was something very real to their faith. These people would not be taking such extraordinary risks without getting something pretty big out of it. Second, it instilled in me a deep love for all things China and Chinese. I came to love the people and their language, gradually feeling at home with them. I even acquired a taste for the food. (Incidentally, it is vastly different from what we find in many Chinese restaurants in the United States.) After I returned home, I began to study the language and martial arts. Some of my Asian friends at the Vineyard church would even quip from time to time that I was more Chinese than they were.

In time, our church initiated a missions partnership with China. We sent small teams to work to train and equip house churches in China and Taiwan. Because Brittany and I were heavily involved in the international ministry at the time, we were in touch with the team members involved. After their first trip, they raved about the incredible experience and strongly encouraged me to join one of the trips. The thought was thrilling; it had been more than fifteen years since I had been to China. I wanted to go so badly.

I distinctly remember a conversation I had with one of the pastors who was urging me to go. I remember these words coming out of my mouth: "I would love to go, but I am a broke, married graduate student. I cannot afford to spend a couple thousand dollars on a ten-day mission trip, but if God gives me the money to go, I will go."

Ever have a moment where God flags in your memory something that you said? Something you probably should not remember, but you absolutely do? That is exactly what happened later with that phrase—although I did not realize it at the time. I had just unknowingly made a deal with God that He planned to take me up on.

All of this occurred in the fall of 2007. Later that spring, God cashed in on my offer.

In the physics department, we concluded our school year with a luncheon for the graduate students who had been awarded in some way during the school year. The luncheon included a program during which a few scholarships were handed out and the teaching assistants who were reviewed well by their students were celebrated. As a teaching assistant who was usually ranked well by my students, I was not surprised when I got an invitation to the luncheon.

The day of the luncheon, I took my seat, mostly excited to eat a catered meal. (Graduate student food is not very good.) As I enjoyed my meal, the program began with the awarding of scholarships. I was not paying much attention, but the next thing I knew, my name was being called. Shocked, I swallowed my last bite, walked to the front of the room and accepted a scholarship I did not even apply for. Then I peeked at the amount—$10,000. What?

It was the last thing I expected. What was even more shocking to me was that it was the first of *four* scholarships given to me that day. I never applied for any of them and did not even know half of them existed. As the luncheon went on, I accepted each award apologetically at the front of the room while the rest of the graduate students glared at me. By the time I left the room, I had been awarded close to $30,000 in scholarship money that I was not at all expecting.

Later, my head was spinning as I walked back to the physics building. *What just happened?* At that moment, I remembered clearly what I had said months before: "If God gives me the money to go, I will go." *Fair enough, God. I said it and You gave me the money. I'll make good on it.*

As soon as I was able, I asked the trip leader to sign me up for the next trip. She told me it would be over Thanksgiving break and asked if that was okay. Knowing this trip was a matter of obedience, I said any time would work.

That summer as we prepared for the trip, I found out that the purpose was to train a group of house church leaders with whom we had recently formed a relationship. This group was a new church plant and eager for any training we could give them. When I asked for more details, however, I learned that we would be training them in prayer for healing.

Oh, no. You've got to be kidding me. Really? This trip? I knew I had to go—to not go would be disobedient—but I was really disappointed since the trip's focus was of little interest to me. *Fine, it's not about me anyway. This is about them. I can go and help with whatever they need, even if it's not what I want to give.*

Resolved to my fate, and with a touch of religiosity, I attended the prayer training course the next time it was offered. I tried my best to actually learn the material, knowing that even though I did not have a personal interest in prayer for healing, I would be teaching it.

Four weeks later I was on a plane to China.

The Kingdom Breaks In

Our healing prayer training for the Chinese leaders came at the end of our week-long schedule. It had been a great time, packed with life-changing experiences. To be back in China was surprisingly rejuvenating to my soul. As we headed to the hotel room to begin the training, I found myself nervously excited. Even though I was not intending to pray for others, I was still slated to teach on Kingdom theology. I had never done training like this before; I was eager for the opportunity. My session was the second of the day. I taught my way through my outline, answered a few questions and returned to my seat thinking I was done.

The next part of the training was the practice session during which the team would demonstrate what we had taught. The plan was to spend time listening for words of knowledge—the kind of leading from the Holy Spirit I saw the pastor doing years ago at the first Vineyard service I attended. We were to spend a few minutes in silence, waiting for impressions or feelings that may be God's direction, then share them with the group and pray for whatever was relevant to God's leading.

As we all sat there trying to listen to the Lord, my attention was mostly on feeling relieved that my part was done. Or so I thought. I began to notice something strange; my left forearm felt odd. It was not quite a pain, just an unusual sensation, and it was coming from *inside* my arm. What was clear was that I had not felt this before, and it was growing stronger. *That's the weirdest thing.*

As I stared at my arm, I recalled a concept from the training class called a sympathy pain. The idea is that God shares a sensation with you that someone else is having for real. This gives you a starting point for prayer. I know it sounds weird—that is exactly what I thought—but there I was experiencing the very thing I had been taught.

When we concluded our listening time, the team leader asked if there were any leadings. I spoke up and asked if someone had a problem with their left forearm. One of the house church leaders shared that she had sprained her wrist about six months earlier and it had not healed correctly. The doctors were not sure what was happening.

My statistical analysis collapsed. *Wow. That's not something that happens regularly in a room of only fifteen people. Probability is not really with that one, huh?*

As I sat there pondering what had happened, the team leader announced that since I had received the direction, I would be the one to model praying for this young woman in front of the whole group.

What? I have no idea what I'm doing. I don't do this stuff or even believe this stuff.

It was too late. There was nothing else to be done other than jump in and try it, and so, reluctantly, jump in I did. After a short interview with the woman to understand her circumstances, I invited the presence of the Holy Spirit.

Now, this next part gets a little crazy, so I want to remind you that this all happened in the context of me not wanting it, not believing it and not pursuing it. Everything I describe next happened in spite of me.

When I invited the Holy Spirit to bring His presence into the room, the last thing I expected to happen did happen. He came. I felt a presence crash through the ceiling directly above the young woman and cascade all over her. It felt powerful, like a waterfall hitting the rocks below. When that presence came upon her, she buckled and dropped straight downward, falling into a heap on the floor. Simultaneously, the people watching in a circle around us responded as well. As far as I could tell, about half of them took a deep gasp as the Spirit entered the room, and three or four of them fell to the ground in various ways. The room that ten seconds earlier was a classroom now looked like a war zone.

Confused and reeling, I tried to take in everything that was happening. The room had exploded into a cacophony of sound as people were now standing, lying down, weeping, praying and more. I heard a confusing noise behind me and looked over my shoulder to see a young woman doubled over on the ground, throwing up into a trash can. *Yikes. I have no idea what that means, but that can't be good.*

My attention was caught back to the woman in front of me. I crouched down, my hand still on her shoulder, and noticed she had an enraged demeanor. She was twisting her body and trying to pull my hand off her shoulder. She began to growl, and while I could not understand what she was saying in Chinese, I could tell it was angry and possibly violent.

"What on earth is happening?" I asked the team leader, shocked and confused.

"It's a demon," she replied matter-of-factly.

"It's a *what?*" I asked, fearing her answer.

"She's manifesting a demon," she responded.

They didn't mention demons in my class!

I was so far in over my head, I had no idea what to do. The team leader apparently expected me to continue leading this thing that had happened unexpectedly on my watch. I began to rack my brain. *What did Jesus do to deal with demons?* Fortunately, I had spent a lot of time in the Bible. Everything I could remember involved Jesus telling the demons to leave. It was all I had, so I commanded that demon to leave the young woman, in Jesus' name.

I wish I could tell you that the spirit left immediately, but that would be far from true. The fact is, it took at least an hour of back-and-forth before the demon left. The battle was not won with power as much as with patience. The woman alternated between lucid thought and manifesting the demon, which would speak and act through her. For some reason, I knew to stick with it and keep pressing forward, and that is what I did. Eventually, she opened her eyes in shock and exclaimed in Chinese, "It's gone! That dark presence I feel is gone!"

Unsure what else to do, I suggested she check out her wrist. It was healed. No one in that room was more shocked than I. Later that afternoon, we cast a demon out of another young woman. The Lord gave her a vision and called her to be a missionary. My life was forever changed.

A Course Redirect

Returning home, I had a lot to process. I still did not like or even understand the packaging of the supernatural experience, but one thing I was absolutely certain of: I saw God step into two people's lives and change them profoundly. I had always been passionate about seeing God change lives, and I had just seen it happen in the deepest way imaginable. I had lots of questions, but I knew I had to see God step into more people's lives and rewrite their stories.

The next few years saw a new trajectory in my life. I knew Jesus and His salvation, but now I began to get to know the Holy Spirit and the Kingdom. I took every training class I could find, sought every mentor, attended every conference or seminar, read tens of thousands of pages and practiced the ministry of the Kingdom everywhere I could. I learned to prophesy, heal the sick, drive out demons and more. I eventually began to train others to do the same. Eventually, I was called to pastoral ministry.

A few years after that, our church started a School of Kingdom Ministry. It now partners with churches around the world. We have trained and equipped thousands of everyday people to continue the supernatural ministry of Jesus. Oh, and in case you are curious, I did complete my physics Ph.D. along the way.

Looking back, I see that while my journey was unique in the way God interrupted my life dramatically, my point of need was far from unique. At the time, I did not even know how to express it, but before His Kingdom came crashing into my life, I was trying to ignore a nagging doubt questioning if my faith actually made any difference to the world around me.

From my Bible studies, I knew that God wants more of us. Jesus often made convicting statements indicating He expects fruit from our faith:

> "You are the light of the world. A city set on a hill cannot be hidden. Nor do people light a lamp and put it under a basket, but on a stand, and it gives light to all in the house. In the same way, let your light shine before others, so that they may see your good works and give glory to your Father who is in heaven."
>
> Matthew 5:14–16

The call of Jesus is always to "come and follow." He calls us to Himself, to know Him and follow the way of life that He demonstrates for us. We hold this true in our lives when it comes to our character and our heart toward others, but sometimes we let ourselves off the hook when it comes to our impact on the world around us. Make no mistake—Jesus changed the world more than any person before or since. To follow Him is to follow the world changer, and we cannot follow everything He modeled unless we are also changing the world.

My faith was never meant just for me, but before this journey, I am not sure I could have pointed to places where my faith had made a difference to the world. Sure, my faith helped me get through my days (some better than others), but how well was I shining as a light in the darkness? How well was the world feeling my influence? How well was God's anointing seeing a return on investment in the world around me?

God challenges each of us in the same ways; if you do not believe me, read the parable of the talents in Matthew 25:14–30 or Luke 19:11–27.

My experience tells me that many of us resonate with this message. We *want* to know our faith makes a difference. You would not be reading this if you did not want to know. You are making your way through these words because you believe you can move into more than what you presently have. Our heart's desire is to live out everything that God calls us to.

The problem is not our desire or lack of effort; it is that we do not know *how* to make a difference. What can we do that changes the world around us? How does it work? What fuels a faith that causes Kingdom impact?

Our journey in these pages begins with working to understand the Gospel message more closely. Our faith is an overflow of the good news of the Gospel. If we want to change the world, therefore, we need to understand how the overflow of our faith impacts the world around us. It turns out that faith that changes the world is hardwired into the Gospel message itself, and so it is vital to get in touch with that first.

Once we understand the *message*, we need to understand the *method*. Changing the world is not something we do out of our own resources or abilities; God knows we cannot do it on our own. He calls us to the impossible, but only because He wants to be with us throughout the process. God intends for us to impact the world by working in partnership with Him.

So, what does it look like to partner with God? What does it look like to bring His resources to the problems around us? We will explore these very questions as we continue our journey through these pages.

Finally, we need to understand the *mission field*. God's redemptive plan is far broader and more expansive than many of us realize. We often focus on individuals. Of course, God is interested in individuals, but He is also working to redeem nations. We need to understand how we cooperate with God's plan to overhaul our lives individually and society as a whole.

My life has been dramatically changed in the years since the Kingdom of God came crashing through that hotel ceiling. I no longer wrestle with the feeling of fruitless faith; instead, I feel the need to stay on my A game and keep up with everything God is doing. My life is now a glorious out-of-control adventure, every day filled with wonder and awe at what God will do next. I have been caught up in God's mission, and I believe God wants the same to happen for you.

It is possible to have faith that changes the world. It is possible to have fruit from the Gospel that you can point to as God's work in and through your life. It is possible to live knowing your life is ringing with eternal significance as you follow the world-changing Jesus. Let us leave our stale faith behind and undertake the journey of Kingdom impact.

IMPACT POINTS

- The Kingdom may come crashing into your life when you least expect it.
- We cannot fully follow Jesus as the world changer without expecting our faith to change the world around us.
- Our journey of Kingdom impact will take us through the message of the Kingdom of God, the method of partnering with the Holy Spirit and the mission field of transforming both individuals and society.

JESUS' MESSAGE AND MODEL

NOW THAT I HAVE ENTERED the realm of parenting, I have discovered the joy of "some assembly required." Today's toys, gadgets and furniture come with dozens of pieces carefully labeled and accompanied by instruction booklets that are complicated enough to make even a well-educated scientist-turned-pastor doubt his salvation.

One of the most frustrating episodes happened a few years ago when we purchased a set of bunk beds for my two older children. I knew I would need some help to stack the beds, so I recruited my dad and brother to join me. We brought all the pieces upstairs, got out the tools and set about assembling. The bottom bed went together easily, and we rejoiced at our quick pace. Perhaps this project would come together smoothly after all.

But alas, it was not to be. The top bunk turned out to be significantly more menacing. All seemed to be going well until we affixed the side railings. They did not fit the way they should. We verified the instructions and realized it was *impossible* to fit them as the instructions depicted.

We retraced our steps and discovered we had put the slats in backward. It was getting close to lunchtime now—low blood sugar always compounds a bad situation—so I quickly disassembled the slats and reinstalled them as shown, but they still did not look right. Upon closer examination, I saw that I needed to flip them, not rotate them. When we finally got those on right, we realized we had put them on wrong on the first bed. Back to work on that one. All said and done, a project that we should have finished in an hour took three hours.

The main problem was that we did not follow the directions closely. Everything was coming together so well; why bother with fuzzy pictures and tiny print? We are guys, right? We can figure this stuff out. *Famous last words.* Those beds came with an instruction booklet for a reason. It showed the details of how everything fits together. Without it, we were stuck in a cycle of failure, trying and re-trying, banging our heads against a wall until we figured it out. We eventually got there, but it was unnecessarily painful.

Ever since the bunk bed fiasco, I have been paying much closer attention to those booklets.

Our journey of faith is similar. There are many facets to living out our faith. An instruction booklet detailing what it means to live a faith engaged with the world can save needless frustration and headaches. Fortunately, we have a model for how it all fits together. The Father did not send a picture in a booklet, though. Instead, He sent a different Word—His Son Jesus. He is the model for fully living out our faith. If we want to work out how our faith is meant to bear fruit through our lives into others, looking at Jesus is the place to start.

Jesus' Primary Message

To understand Jesus' model, we have to understand His message. The two are deeply linked. What was His message? The gospels leave little doubt as to the focus of Jesus' preaching and teaching; it was the Kingdom of God. This was the clarion call at the beginning of His ministry.

> Now after John was arrested, Jesus came into Galilee, proclaiming the gospel of God, and saying, "The time is fulfilled, and the kingdom of God is at hand; repent and believe in the gospel."
>
> Mark 1:14–15

It was the message that He took everywhere.

> But he said to them, "I must preach the good news of the kingdom of God to the other towns as well; for I was sent for this purpose."
>
> Luke 4:43

It was His teaching application for His parables.

> And he said, "With what can we compare the kingdom of God, or what parable shall we use for it?"
>
> Mark 4:30

It is to be the highest priority of our lives.

> But seek first the kingdom of God and his righteousness, and all these things will be added to you.
>
> Matthew 6:33

It is the birthright of those who have been born again.

> Jesus answered him, "Truly, truly, I say to you, unless one is born again he cannot see the kingdom of God."
>
> John 3:3

It is the motivation to avoid sin.

And if your eye causes you to sin, tear it out. It is better for you to enter the kingdom of God with one eye than with two eyes to be thrown into hell.

Mark 9:47

It was illustrated by His miraculous ministry.

But if it is by the Spirit of God that I cast out demons, then the kingdom of God has come upon you.

Matthew 12:28

Finally, it was the message with which He sent out His disciples.

And he called the twelve together and gave them power and authority over all demons and to cure diseases, and he sent them out to proclaim the kingdom of God and to heal.

Luke 9:1–2

The Kingdom of God was truly the focus of Jesus' ministry.[1] It was not the only thing He talked about, but it was certainly the center from which everything else flowed. As we understand His message, we will come to see why Jesus' expression of faith was so transformational to the world around Him.

Unpacking the Kingdom

Much of today's thinking about the Gospel focuses on salvation instead of the Kingdom, so it is easy to blur the two concepts. The Kingdom of God is often understood as referring to eternity or perhaps the group of people who are destined to inhabit eternity—the Church.

This comes about because, in English, the word *kingdom* is usually associated with a geographic region. The United Kingdom, for example, refers to a set of territories under a common rule. In general, when people speak of their "kingdom," they mean the boundaries within which their authority applies, be it a business, property or other entity. As a result, the term "Kingdom of God" comes to mean a region of God's rulership, and the two obvious regions are heaven—the place of His rule—and the Church—the people submitted to His rule.

To the Jews in the first century, however, the Kingdom of God had a distinct meaning apart from heaven or the Church. Jesus understood this; He knew how they were interpreting His message, and He taught using their definition.

One of the clearest Scriptures that illustrates the Jews' understanding of "kingdom" is found in one of Jesus' parables. Luke 19:11–24 tells the story of three servants entrusted with different investments and asked to increase the initial capital. They perform differently and are rewarded accordingly. The context of the parable illustrates the meaning of the Kingdom as Jesus intended it. "He said therefore, 'A nobleman went into a far country to receive for himself a kingdom and then return'" (Luke 19:12).

So, the nobleman goes to another country to receive a kingdom, but then he returns. This is puzzling behavior if the man is receiving a realm to rule over; why would he go get a kingdom and then return? If he went to receive a realm, he would plan to stay in the realm of his rulership. A few verses later, however, we see what is happening. "But his citizens hated him and sent a delegation after him, saying, 'We do not want this man to reign over us'" (Luke 19:14).

The man's enemies protest his agenda because they do not want to be ruled. In other words, what the man leaves to receive is not a country but the *rulership itself*. A kingdom does not describe the territory but rather the means to rule that territory.[2]

This definition makes more sense when we examine Jesus' life and ministry. Jesus does not announce that God's country has arrived but rather that His rulership is imminent.[3] God's rule is active here on earth, and God is about to step into your life and rewrite your story. It is a message of *activity*, a message indicating action. Jesus is not bringing a truth to be acknowledged but the announcement of present reality.

To the first-century Jew, hearing "the Kingdom of God is at hand" would register as, "God is about to flex His God-muscles in your life. Get ready to see Him change things." It is the announcement of a new reality—something big is about to happen. Jesus is, in effect, grabbing people by the shoulders and shaking them out of their stupor, arresting their belief that God is distant and uninvolved or that God is far away and occupied with better things. Jesus is proclaiming the end to this frame of mind. Instead, God is close, involved and taking action. Jesus' message is this: Abandon the old and get on board with this radically new reality.[4]

It is not difficult to see how this message flows into an engaged faith that expects action. Think about it: What would it look like to believe this message down to the core of your being? To believe as Jesus did? To fully believe that God's activity was in a new season? That He was exercising His God-ness in people's lives? That He was so close, you could reach out and touch Him? Suddenly, every moment would be pregnant with the possibilities of heaven, knowing that God could break in *now*, that His power is ready to invade. All of life would be lived in anticipation of His divine incursion into our lives.

This is why Jesus' miraculous ministry is often paired with His message of the Kingdom. "And he went throughout all Galilee, teaching in their synagogues and proclaiming the gospel of the kingdom and healing every disease and every affliction among the people" (Matthew 4:23).

Of course, for this message of God's active rule to have any credibility, things must happen. When God's rulership is introduced into a broken and fallen world, the world cannot remain the same. Indeed, we see that as Jesus proclaims the Kingdom message, the very activity He is describing is taking effect. Jesus is not doing signs to prove His message is accurate; rather, the reality He is proclaiming is manifesting. Where sickness or affliction has a measure of dominion in someone's life, God's reign displaces that sickness and brings the person back to God's created design, which is health. The message and the method are one and the same.

Believing What Jesus Believed

Before we continue, I want to circle back to an important point. When Jesus calls us to follow Him, what we believe as truth must submit to that calling. Put another way, our goal is to believe what Jesus believes. Wherever He is, we need to be headed there.

If we are honest with ourselves, I think many of us live closer to the view of God as far off and uninvolved as opposed to what Jesus believes about God's activity in the message He announces. At best, I tend to think in terms of *God might do something* or *We'll see if God does something*, but that uncertainty is not reflected in Jesus' ministry. He was certain to the core of His being that a new reality was intersecting and redefining the existing reality, that God's activity was absolutely present and the most powerful force in the universe. There was no *might* or *we'll see* about it. How do I know? You do not subject yourself to a Roman flogging and crucifixion to further the cause of a kingdom about which you have any uncertainty. Jesus yielded His life, fully confident that the Kingdom would invade this world and return His life. There was no question in His mind.

I tend to carry a picture of God that feels at odds with Jesus' faith. I'm not alone, however. Many of us carry a deistic image of God—one of an absolutely real and powerful God, just not an engaged God—a God who is busy watching the world from afar, not intimately connected and anticipating involvement. This God feels detached, unassertive, a cosmic Dad relaxing in His easy chair as He channel-surfs His way through our lives.

I daresay that Jesus would not recognize that picture of a remote God. That is not the Father He knew nor the faith He bestowed.

A big part of my journey since the China trip has been to discard that depiction of God and learn to embrace the picture Jesus presents. For many of us, our journey begins by applying Jesus' message to ourselves, recognizing that our picture of God's involvement in the world is grossly inaccurate. We must follow Jesus' instructions and repent, releasing our false picture of God and asking Him to give us His picture of God.

The good news is that we are not the ones who align our story of God with Jesus' story. We could not do it anyway. Have you ever tried to force yourself to believe something you did not believe? It does not work for me. No, the solution is not forcing your mindset to change but rather yielding to Jesus and allowing Him to change the picture for us. Unless Jesus reveals the Father, we cannot know Him. "All things have been handed over to me by my Father, and no one knows the Son except the Father, and no one knows the Father except the Son and anyone to whom the Son chooses to reveal him" (Matthew 11:27).

It is freeing not to have to carry the weight of your own growth. Instead, we can look to Jesus and ask for His grace to bring us to truth.

Let us just stop right now and ask for it. Take a moment and pray this.

Jesus, I ask that You would reveal to me the Father as He really is. I want to see God through Your picture, Jesus. I struggle to believe the Father is active—that He is close and involved—but I want to. I want to believe God's Kingdom is at hand and not far away. So, I give my picture of God to You, Jesus. Take it and mold it to align with the truth. I ask that You would create conviction in my heart of God's proximity and activity. I ask for the same conviction You have of God's imminent rule over the things in this world.

An Easy Yoke

Let us add one more clarification to Jesus' message before we continue. Notice a paradox. Jesus changed the world by announcing that *someone else* was changing the world. He did not bear the burden of changing the world on His shoulders. Rather, He was the herald of another reality, and that reality was changing the world. Jesus often contrasted His inability with God's activity (see John 5:19 and John 8:28).

This understanding keeps our focus in the right place. Often, when we begin to talk about following Jesus and impacting the world, it is easy to start trying to make things happen on our own, carrying the burden on our shoulders. This is not Jesus' way, though. He did not arrive and announce, "I am here to change the world." Rather, He presented a separate reality of God's Kingdom changing the world. In so doing, Jesus was introducing something greater than Himself, something of which He was a part, something that was changing the world. As such, He was simply the one who knew what was coming, and He was letting everyone else in on the secret.

This is a position of radical dependency. Jesus traveled for three years announcing that change was coming—change that He had no control over. He proclaimed God's impending activity into people's lives, yet He did so without the power to make it happen Himself. Finally, He gave up His own life, believing that this same power would resurrect Him.

I do not always love being in a place of such dependency. I would rather take responsibility to change the world myself so I could control the outcome and make good on my promises. As soon as I do that, however, I find the weight crushing. It is a responsibility I was never designed to bear, and one that Jesus did not bear either. Instead, Jesus was at home in a true *trust* in His Father. He absolutely believed to the core of His being that His Father was doing the heavy lifting and that it was His Father's Kingdom that would change the world. Jesus, then, could take a relaxed, dependent posture. He saw Himself as the passenger and the Father as the one in the driver's seat.

You do not have to change the world. Instead, you get to bear witness to a greater reality just as Jesus did. We do not need to carry the weight of our own faith changing the world. That is too heavy a burden to bear. No, we are part of a reality that transcends us. It is bigger and more powerful than we are, and like Jesus, we are its emissaries. This is the reality that changes the world. We can relax and trust the Father whom Jesus reveals to us. As He does, we experience the freedom of knowing God is the one changing the world. That lifts the burden from our shoulders and allows us to experience what Jesus reveals as the fruit of knowing the Father. "Take my yoke upon you, and learn from me, for I am gentle and lowly in heart, and you will find rest for your souls. For my yoke is easy, and my burden is light" (Matthew 11:29–30).

It is wonderful to enter the freedom of changing the world without carrying the weight of it. God is changing the world; He loves us and invites us into the process, but it is His cause we are entering into. God does not ask us to figure out what the world needs or to change the world through our own ideas or efforts. It is not something God delegates to us to figure out but rather something in which we get invited to participate. Interestingly, as we connect with that cause and it becomes real to us, we find lightness as a product of our dependency on God, and it makes us more effective. The more we can get out of the way, the more fruit we bear, because when our focus is on ourselves, it only shuts things down.

A number of years ago, I was at a conference where the session speaker was training people in how to effectively pray for healing. He gave a word of knowledge about shoulder pain, and a few people came up for prayer. The speaker prayed for them and some were healed, but there was a man who did not seem to improve.

The speaker asked what caused the shoulder injury, and the man said he had been shot in the Vietnam War. As soon as he said this, everyone in the auditorium went into "charismatic mode," stretching out their hands and praying in tongues in a mass outpouring. As they did, I felt the Father whisper to me, *"Pay attention, Putty. He won't get healed."*

"What?" I replied. "Why are you telling me this?"

Sure enough, even though the speaker (along with everyone else) prayed for the man, his shoulder did not improve. I asked God, "What are you trying to show me here, God?" I felt the Lord bring to mind a passage in Galatians.

Are you so foolish? Having begun by the Spirit, are you now being perfected by the flesh? Did you suffer so many things in vain—if indeed it was in vain? Does he who supplies the Spirit to you and works miracles among you do so by works of the law, or by hearing with faith . . . ?

Galatians 3:3–5

The Lord pointed out that the room had responded out of an emotional desire to fix the man. The injury seemed difficult to heal, and without realizing it, the people added their effort to their prayers, hoping to move the healing along. It did not work, however, because the Kingdom never comes through the power of our self-effort. It always comes through yielding in faith and allowing God to move.

While I wish I could say I later had the opportunity to pray for the man, I did not know where to find him. There have been a number of times since when I have caught a group of people spinning into anxiety and have helped them relax and trust in God's goodness. I often see people receive healing after redirecting their focus to God's ability.

Our job is to take responsibility for partnering with God, but we do not have the ability to take responsibility for the power of the Kingdom coming into our world. To do that is to put ourselves in God's seat, trying to control things over which we have no control. We are to take complete responsibility for our partnership with God and let the responsibility for changing the world rest on His shoulders.

The World at War

God's rule does not enter the world uncontested. Jesus' proclamation marked the beginning of a cosmic battle. The Kingdom that He announced was the beginning of God's invasion of the enemy's territory. Jesus clarified this when the Pharisees misunderstood the deliverance ministry. "Knowing their thoughts, [Jesus] said to them, 'Every kingdom divided against itself is laid waste, and no city or house divided against itself will stand. And if Satan casts out Satan, he is divided against himself. How then will his kingdom stand?'" (Matthew 12:25–26).

Jesus made an important point. God's Kingdom is not the only rule active on this planet. Satan has a kingdom too, and he is working to extend his destructive and chaotic rule. Jesus has come to declare spiritual war. His purpose is to tear down Satan's kingdom and establish the Kingdom of God in its place.

"The reason the Son of God appeared was to destroy the works of the devil" (1 John 3:8).

God is here to invade planet earth and overthrow Satan. God is the superior power, binding and plundering the enemy's work. Jesus continued His explanation to the Pharisees by demonstrating that God's power is superior and that God's Kingdom is overthrowing and plundering Satan's kingdom. "But if it is by the Spirit of God that I cast out demons, then the kingdom of God has come upon you. Or how can someone enter a strong man's house and plunder his goods, unless he first binds the strong man? Then indeed he may plunder his house" (Matthew 12:28–29).

The proper context in which to understand the Kingdom of God is conflict. God is not only establishing His rule; He is displacing Satan's rule. Said another way, God's rule is not applied to a blank canvas; instead, it covers the rule of the enemy.

Jesus understood ministry and the world as existing against the backdrop of a great spiritual war. Satan apprehended the rule of this planet, and Jesus came because God was taking it back. "Now is the judgment of this world; now will the ruler of this world be cast out" (John 12:31).

This means we must understand our lives in light of the spiritual battle. Much of the Church has been taught to understand the world through a very different perspective, one in which God is pulling every lever and orchestrating all the events in a great cosmic machine; we assume that any of the events that occur in our lives happen *because* they are God's direct intent. The Kingdom perspective stands at odds with this thinking. Rather than assume all things are falling neatly into God's will, the battle between the two kingdoms means the world is messy at times. As in any war, there are victories and setbacks, heroism and casualties.

This is the context for our spirituality and our mission in the world. Jesus came not only to be the initial invasion but to draft us into the cause with Him. He welcomes us into the mission just as he did His original disciples. He dispatched the twelve disciples first, then seventy-two others later, with the same ministry that He carried. "Whenever you enter a town and they receive you, eat what is set before you. Heal the sick in it and say to them, 'The kingdom of God has come near to you'" (Luke 10:8–9).

To be a believer is to be a soldier in a spiritual battle. We are expected to join the cause of the Kingdom message and partner with God to release His rule on the earth. To do so is to follow Jesus' example.

To learn to do this effectively, we need to take a deeper look at the broader story of God's Kingdom invasion. We know God's rule is breaking into human history, but why was His rule not here in the first place? What are we displacing, and how do Jesus' life, death and resurrection fit into that process? To properly step into our mission, we need to examine these questions, and that is what we will do in the next few chapters.

IMPACT POINTS

- Jesus came proclaiming the message of the Kingdom of God—that God is present and His rule is coming from eternity into the present, thereby intersecting our lives.
- We can trust that God really does want to change the world. He carries the weight of this task; we do not.
- God's Kingdom does not exist in a vacuum; rather, it is displacing the kingdom of Satan. This means our lives are lived in the context of a great spiritual battle. This battle is what Jesus invites His disciples into. It is the mission of our faith.

RESTORING OUR LIVES

EACH OF US experiences "hinge points" in life—events that change the rest of our lives. It could be the day we leave home, for example, or our wedding day. It could be the moment we step into a new career, become a parent or receive a life-changing diagnosis. It could be that crucible moment when we discover what we are made of—a vital part of our true selves. In one way or another, these are pivotal experiences that turn everything in a new direction.

The effect of these hinge points can only be seen when we back up and view the broader scope of our lives. The day I got married, for example, the rest of my life profoundly changed, but at the time I could not see exactly how it changed. It is only by zooming out and looking at the arc of my life that I can see how profoundly my life has differed from what it might otherwise have been. At the time, I thought I knew how marriage would affect my life, but really, I had no idea. When I step back from the trees and view the forest, however, I see how much the rest of my life changed that day.

The power of an event is revealed more clearly in context with the overall story. This is so with Jesus' announcement that God's Kingdom was now present. The story of God and humanity's history had entered a new chapter—but what did that mean? What really changed with Jesus' Kingdom declaration?

To see the change, we must examine the biblical story in its entirety; otherwise we do not have enough information to see how Jesus' proclamation informs our faith today. As we will see, when we back up and look at the broader story, it absolutely informs our faith in the present and fills our faith with a profound sense of purpose and clarity of mission.

The next two chapters step through the story of the Kingdom from two different vantage points: one focused on our individual journeys and the other on the story of societies as a whole. Like two sides of a coin, these are the two sides of the Kingdom story. To get the full picture, we need to explore both.

The Fall of Man

To understand a story, we must start at the beginning and work through its entirety. The story of man begins in the very first chapter of the Bible when God creates humanity as His grand finale.

> Then God said, "Let us make man in our image, after our likeness. And let them have dominion over the fish of the sea and over the birds of the heavens and over the livestock and over all the earth and over every creeping thing that creeps on the earth." So God created man in his own image, in the image of God he created him; male and female he created them. And God blessed them. And God said to them, "Be fruitful and multiply and fill the earth and subdue it, and have dominion over the fish of the sea and over the birds of the heavens and over every living thing that moves on the earth."
>
> Genesis 1:26–28

We see in these verses God's intention for creating us. Humanity is given both an identity, in the image and likeness of God, and a destiny, which is dominion over the earth. God then commissions humankind to multiply and bring the world into submission.

These two ideas are tied together. We are created in the image of the King as His representation to the world, and from that identity comes our purpose, which is to rule as God rules. God rules all creation, including the heavens, and we are given rule over this planet. Notice that the task is to fill the earth and *subdue it*. God created the Garden of Eden (see Genesis 2:8), but the rest of the planet is not orderly yet. It is filled with life, but it is unstructured and chaotic.

Adam and Eve's job, therefore, is to take the template of the Garden of Eden and extend the realm of God's design to the ends of the earth. They are the rulers of the terrestrial domain in partnership with Him.

Notice, however, that when God first makes the garden and releases Adam to work, He clarifies the status of a certain tree in the middle of the garden. "And the LORD God commanded the man, saying, 'You may surely eat of every tree of the garden, but of the tree of the knowledge of good and evil you shall not eat, for in the day that you eat of it you shall surely die'" (Genesis 2:16–17).

The tree of the knowledge of good and evil is toxic to man; eating its fruit will result in death. Unfortunately, as you likely know, this is exactly where things go wrong. The serpent has a conversation with Eve and tricks both Eve and Adam into eating from this tree.

At this point, a whole host of problems are introduced to the world, but the one that matters for our discussion is that a power called "death" enters the world. Now, you and I probably think of death primarily as a biological state—what happens when our body's biochemical processes stop functioning. In the ancient world, though, death was not seen biologically but as a spiritual power that was active in the world. This is the kind of thinking we see, for example, in the book of Revelation when Death is thrown into the lake of fire (right after Satan).

> And the sea gave up the dead who were in it, Death and Hades gave up the dead who were in them, and they were judged, each one of them, according to what they had done. Then Death and Hades were thrown into the lake of fire. This is the second death, the lake of fire.
>
> Revelation 20:13–14

You do not throw a biological state into the lake of fire; you throw a spiritual being into the lake of fire. This clarifies Genesis 2:17—God is not saying that Adam's body will run out of steam but rather that Death itself will come after him and rule over him. God is warning Adam and Eve that there is another spiritual power that they cannot defend themselves against, and that eating of the tree will release that power into the world. Paul echoes and expounds on this.

> Therefore, just as sin came into the world through one man, and death through sin, and so death spread to all men because all sinned . . . Yet death reigned from Adam to Moses, even over those whose sinning was not like the transgression of Adam, who was a type of the one who was to come.
>
> Romans 5:12, 14

Adam and Eve sin and fling the door open for death to enter the world. Because everyone in the world eventually sins, death gets its clutches on everyone. Sin is what grants death access, which is why "the wages of sin is death" (Romans 6:23). Humanity, the intended rulers on earth, now becomes the ruled. Death has hijacked the human race and comes for us all.

Let us return to one more element of Genesis 2:17. Notice the language: "the day that you eat of it." The day Adam and Eve eat the fruit, death introduces its power into their lives. The final act of death is the taking of their physical bodies, but the power of death begins to act on them immediately. There are more ways to die than just physically. Notice Paul's description of the pre-salvation state of man. "And you were dead in the trespasses and sins in which you once walked, following the course of this world, following the prince of the power of the air, the spirit that is now at work in the sons of disobedience" (Ephesians 2:1–2).

The first death is internal and spiritual. Adam and Eve die inwardly, and every person born since is born with that same situation. From the inside out, death begins to afflict their lives. It happens relationally as Adam and Eve turn on each other, and it continues as their family eventually breaks down in hatred and murder. It happens vocationally as the God-given gifts of childbearing and farming are cursed and become burdensome. It happens emotionally as they are exiled from the garden and blocked from returning to the place of God's presence. In time, it happens physically as their bodies succumb to death's power.

Adam and Eve's disobedience concerning the tree of the knowledge of good and evil results in the upending of their calling. They are meant to be the rulers of the planet, extending God's rule into realms still dominated by chaos. Instead, they become the ones who are overcome by the forces of chaos and brokenness. The very things they have been sent to extinguish are now empowered to dominate them.

This is the *personal fall*. Satan, through death, gains rule over us and subjects us to his cruel reign. "The thief comes only to steal and kill and destroy" (John 10:10).

Satan is destroying our lives with his power, sending sickness, pain, heartache and death. He is working to break down our relationships and starve our finances. The more his rule is enforced in our lives, the more our lives conform to the pattern of hell. His goal is to drain the entirety of our lives into the pit for eternity.

Light into Darkness

All is not lost, however. As promised, Jesus enters the scene announcing the message of the Kingdom of God. In light of the personal fall, we see the Kingdom message as a challenge to Satan's dominion that corrupts our lives through the power of death. Jesus has indeed come because God intends to overthrow the enemy and return us to living under God's dominion. "He has delivered us from the domain of darkness and transferred us to the kingdom of his beloved Son" (Colossians 1:13).

For Satan's rule over us to be broken, Jesus needs to release us from the power of death. To do so, Jesus invades the world with a new power—the power of life. Nearly everything Jesus teaches is about the power of life—a life from eternity, an eternal life. In the Scriptures, this concept is not directly about the afterlife, although that exists too, but about a life from eternity that is disrupting the power of death on this planet.

John opens his gospel by bringing us back to Creation and reminding us that all things were created through God's Word. "In the beginning was the Word, and the Word was with God, and the Word was God. He was in the beginning with God. All things were made through him, and without him was not any thing made that was made" (John 1:1–3).

With that context established, John lets us know that our experience of darkness is because we do not have Jesus' life. Light is now coming into the world to bring us life and restore us to light. "In him was life, and the life was the light of men. The light shines in the darkness, and the darkness has not overcome it. . . . The true light, which gives light to everyone, was coming into the world" (John 1:4–5, 9).

Satan may rule through the power of death, but Jesus—the Creator—arrives with the power of life to overthrow the power of death and restore creation to its intended design. Jesus is releasing a new creation, one not under the bondage of death but filled with His life.

Jesus' ministry of the Kingdom consists of life overthrowing death. This is what is happening when Jesus brings healing to the sick and freedom to the oppressed. The ultimate expression of His ministry, however, is His resurrecting the dead, a direct statement that the power of His life triumphs over the rule of death. The Kingdom comes bearing the power of life over the work of death. To complete the verse we introduced before: "The thief comes only to steal and kill and destroy. [Jesus] came that [we] may have life and have it abundantly" (John 10:10).

The life that Jesus brings into the world cannot be overcome. I love how the writer of Hebrews describes Jesus' qualifications to be our high priest. "[Jesus] has become a priest, not on the basis of a legal requirement concerning bodily descent, but by the power of an indestructible life" (Hebrews 7:16).

Jesus came with an indestructible life that nothing could overcome. The message we should get from His ministry is that the life of the Kingdom is enough to deal with any problem or situation. There is nothing too big for the life Jesus brings to earth.

We see this overcoming, eternal life in action throughout Jesus' ministry, but let us return to an earlier issue: How does Jesus release *us*—our very lives—from Satan's grip of death?

Entering Eternity Early

Understanding Jesus' crucifixion and resurrection is vital. To be light into our lives, Jesus challenged the work of the enemy and displaced the work of darkness, but that is not the same as delivering us from the dominion of death. If Jesus had not died and resurrected, we would not be free from the power of death.

Jesus delivers us from the power of death by taking us through death with Him. The crucifixion and resurrection are how Jesus walked into the power of death and came out the other side. He was able to do this because His eternal life was too powerful to be bound by death. Jesus did not skirt the power of death; He walked through it unscathed—upgraded, actually—and He brings those who believe in Him along the journey with Him.

> But God, being rich in mercy, because of the great love with which he loved us, even when we were dead in our trespasses, *made us alive together with Christ*—by grace you have been saved—and raised us up with him and seated us with him in the heavenly places in Christ Jesus.
>
> Ephesians 2:4–6, emphasis added

We are freed from death by being made alive together with Christ. Jesus met us in death so that He may bring us into life. Death has no more hold on us because *we have already died*. This is a common theme throughout the New Testament:

> For if we have been united with him in a death like his, we shall certainly be united with him in a resurrection like his.
>
> Romans 6:5

> I have been crucified with Christ.
>
> Galatians 2:20

> For you have died, and your life is hidden with Christ in God.
>
> Colossians 3:3

> But we see him who for a little while was made lower than the angels, namely Jesus, crowned with glory and honor because of

the suffering of death, so that by the grace of God he might taste death for everyone.

Hebrews 2:9

Death worked its best on Jesus, exhausting its power, yet Jesus was resurrected because the power of His life was indestructible. The life He was raised to is beyond the dominion of death, and that means our life in Him is also indestructible.

We know that Christ, being raised from the dead, will never die again; death no longer has dominion over him. For the death he died he died to sin, once for all, but the life he lives he lives to God. So you also must consider yourselves dead to sin and alive to God in Christ Jesus.

Romans 6:9–11

The way we process the death and resurrection of Jesus, therefore, is rather straightforward. We look at Him and say, "That was me too." Jesus demonstrates the quality of the life He brings by dipping it into the power of death, only to have it come out the other side victorious. In so doing, Jesus takes our own lives through the power of death that ruled over us, and He brings us into eternal life. His death was necessary, therefore, to bring us into His life. "And as Moses lifted up the serpent in the wilderness, so must the Son of Man be lifted up, that whoever believes in him may have eternal life" (John 3:14–15).

How do we step into what Jesus did? Jesus repeatedly makes clear that it is only through faith. We do not have the ability to break ourselves out of the power of death; it is only by receiving life from Jesus that we can move from death to life. Only if we believe that Jesus has gone through the power of death can we look to Him to receive the same for ourselves. "Because, if you confess with your mouth that Jesus is Lord and believe in your heart that God raised him from the dead, you will be saved. For with the heart one believes and is justified, and with the mouth one confesses and is saved" (Romans 10:9–10).

Through faith, Jesus' resurrection is *our* resurrection. We have been brought through death into life (see Romans 6:13), and because the lordship of death was the linchpin of Satan's rule over us, this dissolves his hold on us. The enemy's hold over us is broken, and the crumbling of Satan's rule begins.

> Since therefore the children share in flesh and blood, he himself likewise partook of the same things, that through death he might destroy the one who has the power of death, that is, the devil, and deliver all those who through fear of death were subject to lifelong slavery.
>
> Hebrews 2:14–15

Because Jesus experienced death for us, we are liberated from our slavery to death and come into the power of life. Rather than living with the fear of death—a spiritual awareness of the power of death ruling over us—we now live with the fear of the Lord that leads to life. In His own death and life, Jesus joined us in death to bring us into His eternal life. To those of us in Christ, even physical death has been converted to the moment of entering supreme life. As Paul puts it, our mortality is "swallowed up by life" (2 Corinthians 5:4).

Now we come to an interesting point. Those of us who follow Jesus have entered eternity early. The biblical perspective on death is that it is the transition point between this life and the next. We live a life here on earth, then we die and cross over into eternity. Let us take that idea, however, and add the biblical assertion that those of us in Christ have already died. This means we have already crossed the bridge into eternity. Let us look at this passage:

But as it is, [Jesus] has appeared once for all at the end of the ages to put away sin by the sacrifice of himself. And just as it is appointed for man to die once, and after that comes judgment, so Christ, having been offered once to bear the sins of many, will appear a second time, not to deal with sin but to save those who are eagerly waiting for him.

Hebrews 9:26–28

The writer of Hebrews is saying that every person dies once and then is judged, but because Jesus died and was judged for all of us, when Judgment Day comes, there will be nothing left for believers to be judged for because we already live on the far side of judgment. We have been pushed into eternity while still in our mortal bodies. The end of time has already come upon us.

We are people from eternity who are alive in the present. Jesus pushes us through the earthly timeline and plants our lives firmly on the far side of the end of the age. For believers, Jesus is the end of the age, and now we have survived the apocalypse in a world to which it is still coming.

This presents an interesting picture. The end of the age has already happened for Christians. Believers in Christ have crossed over into the future while the rest of the world is still living out its days under the dominion of death. We are rooted in eternity yet still living in the present. We are citizens of a Kingdom not of this world (see John 18:36), walking out our days in a world that is still held captive by the powers of darkness. Yes, we are still in the world, but we are not of this world any longer (see John 17:14).

Our Message and Mission

All of this brings us back to the question at hand: What does Jesus' Kingdom announcement mean to our lives today?

First, we understand that Jesus has become King. He came announcing God's rule, and through His death and resurrection He conquered the power of this world and was crowned the victorious King. "But we see him who for a little while was made lower than the angels, namely Jesus, crowned with glory and honor because of the suffering of death, so that by the grace of God he might taste death for everyone" (Hebrews 2:9).

We proclaim the Kingdom of God through the kingship of Christ. God's rulership is being released on the earth, and Jesus Christ is forever the entry point of that rule. Jesus has received all authority on the earth (see Matthew 28:18), and the life that belongs to Him continues to invade and overthrow the power of death. Jesus demonstrates that His power is victorious over all, and He continues in victory. He has become the human being who is rightfully ruling this planet as God designed.

Our message is that Jesus has conquered the power enslaving this world, and He is making a new creation. While Jesus pointed to the invading power of God's rule, we point to that same rule through the overcoming victory of Jesus on this earth.

> And I heard a loud voice in heaven, saying, "Now the salvation and the power and the kingdom of our God and the authority of his Christ have come, for the accuser of our brothers has been thrown down, who accuses them day and night before our God."
>
> Revelation 12:10

We proclaim that Jesus has become King and He is ruling over the personal evil in our lives. We declare His victory and we look to Him to bring the power of life into the places where the work of death has not yet been dislodged. We announce that the Kingdom invasion is already underway and Jesus has taken the beachhead. We point to His continual invading rule to destroy the works of the enemy.

Second, we understand that our lives are caught up in Jesus' rule because we have been made people of eternity who belong to His Kingdom. Our home is no longer this world but heaven itself; that is where we belong (see Hebrews 13:14). While we may still walk out a portion of our days on earth, in a world still bound through corruption to death, we do not live that way any longer.

It is our responsibility to live consistently in the world. Note the way that Paul frames his instructions on morality: "Do not present your members to sin as instruments for unrighteousness, but present yourselves to God as those who have been brought from death to life, and your members to God as instruments for righteousness" (Romans 6:13).

Paul is essentially saying, "Do not do that other stuff, because it's not who you are anymore." We used to be under the dominion of death, and it was natural for our lives to bear witness to that fact. Now, however, we are people who have been brought into life, and as such, we have a responsibility to walk in the ways of life, not the ways of death. Christian morality is not a matter of "doing the right thing" as much as being faithful to our new home. It is a choice of integrity or hypocrisy with respect to the realm of life in which we now dwell.

Third, it is our responsibility as people of the light to do our part to announce and partner with Jesus' Kingdom as it continues to advance upon the rule of darkness. This is why God asks for fruitfulness from our faith. We have not been saved to sit on the bench and watch the battle around us, but to get in the game. God has drafted us into the invading force, and we have a part to play in this great cosmic drama.

Jesus has now placed us in Him to bring us from death to life (see 1 Corinthians 1:30). Further, He has placed Himself in us that His glory may continue to manifest in this world (see Colossians 1:27). Jesus' rule continues to be exercised through our actions.

He has put Himself in us that we may continue to speak His words and extend His reach. We are the means by which Christ furthers His rule on this planet.

In this way, those of us in Christ are restored to the original design of humanity, extending the rule of God on the earth as He intended. Jesus has established a new Garden of Eden. Through the cross, He becomes the tree of life for us. Adam and Eve chose the tree of the knowledge of good and evil, but when we choose Jesus Christ, by faith we choose the tree of life.[1] We are restored to our full humanity, identity and purpose.

This is what I stumbled into on that mission trip to China. The power of the enemy is still alive and well in the world, causing brokenness, chaos, darkness and bondage. Not a day goes by that we do not encounter destruction in the lives of people around us. We, however, are the ones who have been designed to counter that reality with a better reality. We are the ones God purposed from the beginning to tame the world's chaos and darkness and bring His life and peace to it. "We know that we are from God, and the whole world lies in the power of the evil one" (1 John 5:19).

God's Kingdom is still at hand. The same voice that said "Let there be light" also said that God's Kingdom has arrived and will not be leaving anytime soon. In fact, He furthered that reality and anchored it to the earth with the cross. We now proclaim that this reality has the power to bring Jesus' new-creation life to bear against the work of death in the world around us.

Just yesterday, I was writing an earlier portion of this chapter at a bookstore in town. As I left to go home, a man caught me outside the door and asked for money. Taking one look at him, I could see his lot had been rough lately. I also saw an opportunity to bring life into death, so I stopped and talked with him. I asked him about his life and what was going on. He mentioned having damaged knees and needing knee replacement surgery in a month or two.

I made him a deal. "I'll give you some cash if you'll let me pray for you. What do you think of that?" He readily accepted, and I placed my hand on his knee and prayed, releasing the power of life into his body and commanding his knees to be made whole. After thirty seconds of prayer, I asked him to get up and walk around a bit.

He got to his feet and walked. I could see from his gait that he was still in pain, but he noted that the knee felt halfway better. I prayed again, this time a few short prayers releasing the power of the Kingdom into his knees. I told him to walk around a bit, and this time he was stunned as he walked around with knees feeling considerably better. I could tell from his stride that he was not feeling the previous pain. Jesus' kingship had been established.

The man asked me where I went to church. I filled him in on the details and invited him to come see me there. He embraced me and said he would. Making good on my promise, I gave him all the cash I had on hand and started making my way home with a fresh smile on my face, feeling fulfilled because I knew I had just lived out my purpose on this earth, proclaiming and releasing Jesus' rule into the brokenness in people's lives.

Here is the thing, though. According to the Gospel of the Kingdom, that was no special encounter. It was fun and exciting but by no means a mountaintop experience. I could tell you dozens of similar stories, and I'm far from the only one living out this Kingdom message. On one hand it is supernatural, and on the other hand it is normal. In our journey of faith, the inbreaking Kingdom is not meant to be exceptional but our consistent experience. This is what our faith can look like, because this is what Jesus came to give us—God's Kingdom on earth, extending its rule through us.

IMPACT POINTS

- Satan took humanity captive through deceiving Adam and Eve into releasing the power of death into the world. Since that time, death has had dominion over each of us.

- Jesus overthrows the power of death in our lives by bringing us through death into life. Death no longer has a hold on us because we have already died with Jesus.

- We are now citizens of the realm of life, sent to release life into this world that is still corrupted by death. We are announcing and establishing Jesus' kingship on earth.

RECLAIMING THE PLANET

A FEW YEARS AGO, I visited a friend who was a software engineer at Facebook. The company had recently built an office building—at the time billed as the largest open office building in the world. I was curious to see what a top Silicon Valley office complex would be like.

Coming away from that trip, I can join the words of the Queen of Sheba to King Solomon and say that I was not told the half of it. It sported multiple cafeterias and restaurants that were all free to all the employees, an on-site arcade and fitness center, vending machines dispensing keyboards, headphones and other computer accessories at no cost. And to top it off, the roof was fully gardened, including grown trees. It included a half-mile walking loop and a field large enough for the employees to gather and play Ultimate Frisbee.

As I followed my friend through the various buildings, I was struck by how strongly Facebook's culture permeated everything around me. The complex was saturated with it. Posters espousing Facebook's philosophy adorned every wall. Artwork abounded, announcing events designed to foster the corporate culture.

Facebook even inscribed *Hack* (one of their philosophical approaches) in giant letters in the sidewalk.[1]

The plan to reinforce the culture was definitely working. I saw balloons scattered throughout the building celebrating employees' work anniversaries, and Facebook paraphernalia covered employees' desks. They were so bought in that they freely advertised the company among themselves. It was clear to me that being immersed in a dynamic workplace was a major part of their identity.

I think that's how it works for all of us. A part of ourselves is formed by stories bigger than we are. We want to see ourselves as members of a broader family; this helps us define ourselves. It can be your natural family, your local church family, your alma mater, even the Rotary Club or the sports stadium you attend. We all cherish the places and organizations that help shape the way we see ourselves.

As we saw in the last chapter, the Kingdom story is about Jesus overthrowing the power of death and bringing us into His life. Running parallel to this is also a Kingdom story at a global scope. Yes, Jesus came to rescue each of us, but He also came to inherit the nations. These are the two sides of the same Kingdom of God. They describe the journey from two different angles. To understand our faith and our mission fully, we need to explore this narrative.

One note as we continue: This chapter contains ideas about faith that you may not be used to. The Western church, by and large, has taken an individual-oriented approach to faith. It is my hope that, though this may seem like a strange point, it will lead to an understanding of Scripture in a new light.

A Closer Look at the Kingdom of Darkness

We saw in the last chapter that Satan acquired dominion over humanity through death entering the world. Death, then, became

Satan's right-hand general, stretching its dominion into each of our lives. A corollary of this—one that we did not explore deeply in the last chapter—is that Satan's kingdom is more complex than merely Satan plus demons. The problem is that we think too simply about the organization of the powers of darkness. Because we have not thought carefully about it and because Satan and demons are highlighted in the gospels, we assume that is all there is. Yet this is not how the Bible portrays Satan's forces. It is how the Western church pictures the kingdom of darkness, but that is because most people have not read and thought carefully about the subject. In a number of places, Scripture points to the forces of evil as an organized enterprise.

> Put on the whole armor of God, that you may be able to stand against the schemes of the devil. For we do not wrestle against flesh and blood, but against the rulers, against the authorities, against the cosmic powers over this present darkness, against the spiritual forces of evil in the heavenly places.
>
> Ephesians 6:11–12

Satan and his demons are real, but there is more happening in the spirit realm. We can expect to encounter not only demons but also rulers, authorities, even cosmic powers or spiritual forces in heavenly places. This means that while we can expect evil to have a direct, personal influence, we can also expect evil to have structured, strategic influence. The Kingdom of God is about God's reign displacing both of these evil influences.

To delve deeper, let's examine a major theme in the Old Testament. While the New Testament has a lot to say about individual evil and personal redemption, the Old Testament's focus is often broader in scope. It is primarily a story about God and His nation Israel compared to the other nations of the world and their gods.[2]

While it may seem disconcerting to a westerner, it is important to note that the Bible consistently treats the gods of other nations as real entities. For a long time, I imagined that the foreign nations who worshiped idols were just imagining gods that did not actually exist. That assumption, however, is not biblical.[3] The message of the Old Testament is not that God is real and the other gods are fictional but rather that God is the only true God deserving worship and that He is far superior to these lesser gods.

> Who is like you, O Lord, among the gods? Who is like you, majestic in holiness, awesome in glorious deeds, doing wonders?
>
> Exodus 15:11

> For the Lord your God is God of gods and Lord of lords, the great, the mighty, and the awesome God, who is not partial and takes no bribe.
>
> Deuteronomy 10:17

What are we to think of these gods? The Bible describes them as real spiritual beings in league with Satan and arrayed against the Lord. They crave and are empowered by worship (see 2 Kings 23). They are not in any way equal to God Himself but are divine beings that are active in the cosmic spiritual drama.

The Story of the Nations

To see where this situation of nations and their gods comes from and how it fits in the Old Testament storyline, we have to take a closer look at the events after the flood as depicted in Genesis 8. After bringing Noah and his family safely through the flood, God reiterates His instructions to man to be fruitful and multiply. God then makes a covenant with Noah. What follows is two chapters outlining Noah's descendants and the nations they fostered. It is the story of Noah's family line growing to cover the world just as God commissioned them to do.

Genesis 11 takes a closer look at how the nations were dispersed. The Tower of Babel is an important story because it frames the "God versus gods" theme.

The story starts with the people *not* scattering but instead gathering to build a tower to reach heaven. When the Lord sees their efforts, He is not thrilled with the trajectory of humankind unified in disobedience, so He divides them.

> "Come, let us go down and there confuse their language, so that they may not understand one another's speech." So the Lord dispersed them from there over the face of all the earth, and they left off building the city.
>
> Genesis 11:7–8

Notice God's intent: "Come, let us go down and there confuse their language, so that they may not understand one another's speech" (Genesis 11:7). Who is God referring to when He says "us"? It turns out He is speaking to the spiritual beings that will eventually fall and become the gods of the nations.

God takes these spiritual beings to earth, disperses the people into groups (nations) and assigns each nation to a ruling spiritual being. These "sons of God" are each given a nation, and Israel is the nation that God keeps for Himself. "But the Lord's portion is his people, Jacob his allotted heritage" (Deuteronomy 32:9).

Moses describes it this way: "When the Most High gave to the nations their inheritance, when he divided mankind, he fixed the borders of the peoples according to the number of the sons of God" (Deuteronomy 32:8).[4]

This is why the next chapter in Genesis recounts God's calling of Abraham. These two storylines are meant to be set in contrast—the nations of the world have been dealt out to other spiritual beings, but God chooses Abraham and his descendants directly for Himself. The other nations have been separated from God, but God uses Abraham's lineage to create a nation that will be a blessing to all the other nations that do not have a direct relationship with Him:

> Now the LORD said to Abram, "Go from your country and your kindred and your father's house to the land that I will show you. And I will make of you a great nation, and I will bless you and make your name great, so that you will be a blessing. I will bless those who bless you, and him who dishonors you I will curse, and in you all the families of the earth shall be blessed."
>
> Genesis 12:1–3

Israel is God's chosen nation and the only one that is in direct relationship with Him. Biblically, however, Israel plays a significant role beyond being the "Messiah delivery device." Through Israel, God plans to reach out to every other nation of the world and minister to them.

What happens to these other nations? The gods of these nations begin to crave worship and so violate God's design. When that happens, they fall into evil and perpetuate it. Baal, Dagon, Ashtoreth and other deities start diverting worship toward themselves and away from the Lord. Eventually, they line up against God and join forces with Satan. This is what Satan refers to when he tempts Jesus:

> And the devil took him up and showed him all the kingdoms of the world in a moment of time, and said to him, "To you I will give all this authority and their glory, *for it has been delivered to me*, and I give it to whom I will."
>
> Luke 4:5–6, emphasis added

Satan has aligned behind him not only death but these gods of the nations as well. He is amassing forces of darkness operating at all levels. While death has its grip on individuals, these gods have their grip on *societies*. They are affecting the social, political and economic structures.

Their activities come to light in a passage that seems incredibly odd until we trace the logic we have been outlining in this chapter. In Psalm 82, God summons the gods of the nations and pronounces judgment over them:

> God has taken his place in the divine council; in the midst of the gods he holds judgment: "How long will you judge unjustly and show partiality to the wicked? *Selah.* Give justice to the weak and the fatherless; maintain the right of the afflicted and the destitute. Rescue the weak and the needy; deliver them from the hand of the wicked."
>
> They have neither knowledge nor understanding, they walk about in darkness; all the foundations of the earth are shaken.
>
> I said, "You are gods, sons of the Most High, all of you; nevertheless, like men you shall die, and fall like any prince."
>
> Arise, O God, judge the earth; for you shall inherit all the nations!
>
> Psalm 82

God accuses the gods of the nations of injustice, partiality to the wicked and dismissal of the weak and needy. They have failed to rule righteously and have brought darkness to the nations. What is God's verdict? They will die and God will inherit the nations Himself.

Let's pause here to reflect. This tells us that the social ills of society are the product of more than just fallen humanity or broken systems; they have been sown into society by malevolent spiritual beings. Poverty, for example, is more than a resource problem. There is a spiritual power driving poverty—similarly for racism, slavery, unfair labor practices or dysfunctional systems of justice, education or health care. There are spiritual powers connected to the corruption of society.

One side of the Kingdom story is that of God ruling in our individual lives and countering personal evil. The other side in God's rule, however, is of intersecting and overthrowing societal evil, thereby creating a righteous civilization according to His design for society. God's rule will not have been fully established until both threads have been fulfilled, and so full Kingdom impact involves God's invasion and restoration of personal lives as well as dealing with these broader issues of society as a whole.

For God to rebuild societies as He designed them, the nations need to be reconciled to Him. They need to be delivered from the grip of these foreign gods and restored to God. These fallen gods have an assigned authority that needs to be reclaimed by the Lord.

This line of reasoning may feel new—there is a good chance you have not heard too many sermons on it—but it is a major theme throughout the Bible. This is what Jesus refers to when He talks about heading to the cross. "Now is the judgment of this world; now will the ruler of this world be cast out. And I, when I am lifted up from the earth, will draw all people to myself" (John 12:31–32).

Notice the parallel themes in comparing Jesus' language to Psalm 82: the judgment of the earth/world and Jesus drawing not just the Jews but all people to Himself.[5]

How does that work? How does God inherit the nations? We are about to find out.

The Role of Israel

Have you ever wondered why so much of the Bible is explicitly about Israel? I know I did. If Jesus is the whole point, why is the Old Testament so much longer than the New Testament? Why so much focus on Israel?[6]

Israel's key role in the Scriptures is not apparent because we have not been looking for the story of the nations. Just as God uses Jesus—an individual—to redeem individuals, God uses Israel—a nation—to redeem nations. (We will see later how that brings us to Jesus.) This is why Israel and her history matter so deeply. Israel is the vessel God has chosen to reach the nations and bring them back to Himself.

Consider what Moses shares with the Israelites when God brings them out of Egypt to Mount Sinai. This is the birth of Israel as a nation, the hinge point when God makes His purposes abundantly clear:

> "You yourselves have seen what I did to the Egyptians, and how I bore you on eagles' wings and brought you to myself. Now therefore, if you will indeed obey my voice and keep my covenant, you shall be my treasured possession among all peoples, for all the earth is mine; and you shall be to me a kingdom of priests and a holy nation." These are the words that you shall speak to the people of Israel.
>
> Exodus 19:4–6

God defines three things here that are unique to Israel and stand in contrast with the other nations of the world:[7]

	Israel	Gentile Nations
Nation's Relationship with God	Chosen covenant people	Separated from access to God
Identity as a Nation	God's inheritance: treasured possession of the Lord	Other gods' inheritance: under the rule of foreign gods
Destiny as a Nation	Ministers of the Lord to other nations	Enemies of the Lord

Israel has been uniquely equipped to minister to the nations of the world. As the only nation who knows the true God, her calling is to be God's light in a dark world. This is why God is so insistent on Israel staying pure, not mixing with other nations or being drawn away after foreign gods. To do so is not simply making a mistake; it is being recruited by the other side and crossing battle lines.

Other than the few times in history that Israel was able to minister to the other nations, Israel seems to have failed in fulfilling her calling as a holy nation of priests. She never maintains any traction in following the Lord. She is regularly plagued by idolatry and immorality of every kind. In time, the nation splits into two nations, each is conquered by foreign powers and Judah is exiled to Babylon. This is by design; the implication is that Israel has joined the other peoples of the world at the Tower of Babel.

Even after the exile and the rebuilding of Jerusalem, there is a sense that Israel has not *really* been restored. They return, and even though they rebuild the temple, there is no Ark of the Covenant to put in it. They have the building but not the presence of the Lord. The people who remember the first temple weep aloud when the second one is built, knowing it is but a shadow of what they once had (see Ezra 3:12). A portion of Israel (two tribes) has returned to her land, but she has lost her identity as the chosen people of God with whom His presence rests.

Furthermore, Israel is not *free*. In fact, she is conquered repeatedly by foreign powers. She is economically and militarily oppressed. She is not ruled by the Lord; she is ruled by other nations and their foreign gods. Rather than being God's special nation, she has been downgraded to a portion of the inheritance of these dark powers.

While the Jews did not know it at the time, the New Testament reveals that in all this upheaval, Israel was actually fulfilling her divine purpose. She was destined to become a light to every nation, yet not in her own strength. Like Jesus, she would fulfill the role of the light by first taking the darkness upon herself.

This downward spiral reaches its nadir with Jesus Christ. When Jesus is on trial, the Israelites take the final step into identification with the world and make themselves direct enemies of their own God.

> Pilate said to them, "Then what shall I do with Jesus who is called Christ?" They all said, "Let him be crucified!" And he said, "Why? What evil has he done?" But they shouted all the more, "Let him be crucified!" . . . And all the people answered, "His blood be on us and on our children!"
>
> Matthew 27:22–23, 25

> They cried out, "Away with him, away with him, crucify him!" Pilate said to them, "Shall I crucify your King?" The chief priests answered, "We have no king but Caesar."
>
> John 19:15

The journey is now complete. Israel has become like the other nations of the world. When Jesus dies, He does so not only as our personal Messiah but also as the King of the Jews—Israel's head.[8]

As we have seen, it is not just our lives but society itself that must be liberated from the clutches of the kingdom of darkness. The powers of the gods have their hands wrapped around civilization. For God's rule to be fully established, society itself needs to be freed from evil's grip. To do so, it must die and be resurrected. That is what God did to Israel through Jesus. Israel must be fully identified with the nations and cultures of the world so she can die as their brokenness. This is why even Israel's continual turning astray was part of God's redemptive purpose. Jesus, as the King, is the one who is responsible for Israel as a nation. Jesus dies as the King of Israel and resurrects a new Israel called the Church.

According to the covenant of the law, if Israel was untrue to the covenant, the curses of her failure would come upon her and she would be destroyed (see Deuteronomy 28). When Jesus arrives on earth, Israel has fulfilled the limit of her fallenness. This is why when Jesus comes to Jerusalem, He pronounces not blessing but destruction (see Matthew 23, 24). There was a generation allotted the judgment due them according to Israel's failure, and the clock had hit its limit.

> On you may come all the righteous blood shed on earth, from the blood of righteous Abel to the blood of Zechariah the son of Barachiah, whom you murdered between the sanctuary and the altar. Truly, I say to you, all these things will come upon this generation.
>
> Matthew 23:35–36

Israel was going to be destroyed. Jesus comes and dies as the first portion as the King of Israel. The rest comes when the Romans destroy Jerusalem forty years later in AD 70. The Israel that exists in Jesus, however, resurrects along with Him as a new creation, unlike the natural Israel.

This precipitates the shift in focus from Jew to Gentile as recorded in the New Testament. Originally, Israel was superior among the nations, and for good reason. With Israel's destruction, there are no natural nations in relationship with God any longer; only the Church, the new Israel, is in direct relationship with God. Natural heritage is irrelevant; the deciding factor is whether or not we are part of Jesus' new-creation Israel. "For neither circumcision counts for anything, nor uncircumcision, but a new creation. And as for all who walk by this rule, peace and mercy be upon them, and upon the Israel of God" (Galatians 6:15–16).

Israel now has a different role than we have previously seen. Reborn as the Church, she *became* the sacrificial lamb to the nations and is now the community armed to bring the society of the future into the present world.

Now, if this whole line of reasoning seems bizarre, consider the many verses that discuss this directly. Here are a few.

> Then what advantage has the Jew? Or what is the value of circumcision? Much in every way. To begin with, the Jews were entrusted with the oracles of God. What if some were unfaithful? Does their faithlessness nullify the faithfulness of God?
>
> Romans 3:1–3

The Jews were entrusted with something special from God. They were not faithful to what they were given, but that does not invalidate God's faithfulness to fulfill Israel's purpose. Paul continues:

> But if our unrighteousness serves to show the righteousness of God, what shall we say? That God is unrighteous to inflict wrath on us? (I speak in a human way.) By no means! For then how could God judge the world?
>
> Romans 3:5–6

Paul is saying that God used Israel's unrighteousness to fulfill His purpose. The way of the Lord is always to enter into death that He may bring Kingdom life. Paul continues:

> What shall we say then? Is there injustice on God's part? By no means! For he says to Moses, "I will have mercy on whom I have mercy, and I will have compassion on whom I have compassion."
>
> Romans 9:14–15

> So then he has mercy on whomever he wills, and he hardens whomever he wills.
>
> Romans 9:18

What if God, desiring to show his wrath and to make known his power, has endured with much patience vessels of wrath prepared for destruction, in order to make known the riches of his glory for vessels of mercy, which he has prepared beforehand for glory—even us whom he has called, not from the Jews only but also from the Gentiles?

Romans 9:22–24

In God's divine purpose, Israel was hardened so that she would be the open door not only for the Jews but for the Gentiles as well to enter the mercies of God. Does that mean God has forsaken Israel or that she has failed? Not at all. Paul continues to explain that the people of God are only chosen because Israel was chosen (see Romans 11:16). Natural Israel—the Jews by birth—will also be one of the nations reached by the new Israel, which is the Church.

So I ask, did they stumble in order that they might fall? By no means! Rather, through their trespass salvation has come to the Gentiles, so as to make Israel jealous. Now if their trespass means riches for the world, and if their failure means riches for the Gentiles, how much more will their full inclusion mean!

Romans 11:11–12

One last point on this storyline. When Jesus stands before the Pharisees, He tells them that from now on, they "will see the Son of Man seated at the right hand of Power and coming on the clouds of heaven" (Matthew 26:64). This is incredibly significant because Jesus is quoting Daniel 7. The scene is parallel to Psalm 82, where the authority of the gods of the nations is stripped and given to the Messiah. This is why the Pharisees cry blasphemy at Jesus' declaration.

But the [divine] court shall sit in judgment, and his [the god of Rome's] dominion shall be taken away, to be consumed and destroyed to the end. And the kingdom and the dominion and the greatness of the kingdoms under the whole heaven shall be given to the people of the saints of the Most High; his [the Son of Man's] kingdom shall be an everlasting kingdom, and all dominions shall serve and obey him.

Daniel 7:26–27, additions mine

Jesus is saying that two events will happen simultaneously. While He is being judged and condemned on the earth, the gods of the nations are being judged and stripped of their authority in the heavens. While they remain alive with some power and influence (see Daniel 7:12), they have been removed from their assignment over the nations. That assignment has been transferred to Jesus.

The Community of the Kingdom

All of this means that the Church is the community from eternity. It is not only the community of people from eternity but the community *itself* that lives according to Kingdom rules altogether different from this world. The gods of this world and the broken societies have no hold on us; we are the family that lives from a different age. We are a completely unique thing in this world; there is no other community that is the firstfruits of the kind that exists in heaven. We are not just another social institution; we are the only Kingdom institution.

As such, we are uniquely qualified to reach the world with the eternal life that we can access. The world does not have the tools to solve its problems. We do. Only the Church has the spiritual authority to deal with the roots of the issues facing the world. Only we have God's righteous society in our midst. The natural world may be able to generate solutions that alleviate the immediate problems, but the inherent causes are spiritual problems requiring spiritual *and* physical solutions. The Church alone has the solutions for the real problems in the world.

The gods of the world have not ceased to exist. They still work to affect our natural world through ideologies, philosophies (see Colossians 2:8) and social structures. At times, we can even trace their presence through history. The goddess Ashtoreth in the Old Testament (see 1 Kings 11:5) was known in other cultures as Astarte and to the Greeks as Aphrodite. In every case, she was a goddess of lust, one who is still present in our day of rampant pornography and sexual deviance. Molech, a god who hungers for child sacrifice (see Leviticus 18:21), is likely well pleased with the more than fourteen million abortions that have been reported in the United States since its legalization in 1970. Jesus Himself warns us of the god Mammon (see Matthew 6:24), who longs for greed and the selfish use of money. It is not hard to see his presence in our day.

Society at large will continue to work on the various social issues that arise, but the best they can do is treat the symptoms. Only the Church—the community of heaven—has the power to break cultures loose from these spiritual authorities. That is the task assigned to us. Luke is hinting at this when he includes the episode in Acts 19 of people rioting in Ephesus because worship of the goddess Artemis is in decline:

> And there is danger not only that this trade of ours may come into disrepute but also that the temple of the great goddess Artemis may be counted as nothing, and that she may even be deposed from her magnificence, she whom all Asia and the world worship.
>
> Acts 19:27

The subtext is this: Another one bites the dust. Another power is toppled by the rule of Jesus. God's plan is to use the Church to pry the world loose from the grip of every illegal power. Jesus has received the ultimate victory and has established the new age in which every power is subjected to Him. We, the Church, the community of that age, get to live out the freedom and fullness we have in Christ.

> What is the immeasurable greatness of his power toward us who believe, according to the working of his great might that he worked in Christ when he raised him from the dead and seated him at his right hand in the heavenly places, far above all rule and authority and power and dominion, and above every name that is named, not only in this age but also in the one to come. And he put all things under his feet and gave him as head over all things to the church, which is his body, the fullness of him who fills all in all.
>
> Ephesians 1:19–23

This is what it means for God's Kingdom to enter our world. It means freedom and deliverance from personal evil and societal evil. It means we get to be both *individuals* and *a people* of the future—human beings who belong to a new creation, bringing the powers of this Kingdom to bear on the problems of this world, living in this world and introducing it to the way society works in the new age. The power of God's invading rule has redefined us, both as individuals and as a community. Now we get to live as signposts, introducing others to the new reality of the Kingdom of God.

How do we fulfill that calling? We will explore this in greater detail, but the short answer is that we do so by being intentional to release the culture of the future into the present.[9] As others enter our fellowship, the Kingdom leavens the world. "And again he said, 'To what shall I compare the kingdom of God? It is like leaven that a woman took and hid in three measures of flour, until it was all leavened'" (Luke 13:20–21).

The Church is called to fulfill Israel's calling because we are Israel, resurrected and completed in Jesus. Now we are called to be the light to the nations. Now we are the unique possession of the Lord, called to minister to a world that belongs to Jesus but is still held by the powers of darkness. Israel has borne the burden of the brokenness of the world. Now every nation can come under the rule of Jesus Christ through His body. He is the tree of life and the source of healing for the nations (see Revelation 22:2). We, the new Israel, are now the chosen people, the nation of God's own possession, the royal priesthood. "But you are a chosen race, a royal priesthood, a holy nation, a people for his own possession, that you may proclaim the excellencies of him who called you out of darkness into his marvelous light" (1 Peter 2:9).

IMPACT POINTS

- The Bible speaks not only of personal evil but also of societal evil. The social ills in our nations are seeded and cultivated by dark spiritual powers.

- God redeemed societies with a new society. Israel is called to be the Lord's inheritance to reach the nations of the world.

- In Jesus, Israel died and was resurrected as a community of the new creation called the Church. The Church has been freed from the powers of this world and is now sent to liberate the rest of the world from the social evil perpetrated upon it.

A WORLD AT WAR

THERE IS SOMETHING deep within us that is programmed to hate betrayal. Of all the offenses that can be committed, betrayal is one of the most grievous. Treason, a close cousin to betrayal, is often a capital offense. We even make examples out of infamous betrayers to show how strongly we detest their actions. (Benedict Arnold, anyone?)

I believe God has made our despising of betrayal strong because we are made to combat the original traitor, Satan, and his kingdom of darkness. Satan was the first narcissist—so in love with himself that he chose himself over God and His ways.

As we have seen, in his attempt to usurp God, Satan created a second *kingdom*—a rule that was in opposition to God's. Even though God cursed him and cut him down after his transgression in the Garden of Eden, he recruited allies. Death itself and the gods of the nations of the world joined him to dismantle God's creation. These two kingdoms have been at war ever since.

Jesus leads the charge of the Kingdom of God—a kingdom defined by love, light, hope and freedom. The enemy battles to maintain fear, control, injustice, loss and death. These two spiritual forces clash every day. Indeed, we live our lives with this invisible spiritual war as the backdrop of our existence. The battle lines intersect every aspect of society, including our individual lives.

When God steps into a situation, He conforms it to His design. The sick are healed, the demonized are set free, the broken are comforted and the oppressed are liberated. People come to know the Lord, and justice and mercy reign. Freedom rings in the air and poverty is eradicated. This is the Kingdom and the action of God's will in our lives.

At the same time, the enemy is working to release his will in our lives, causing a withering of all that is good and true. Our lives are pillaged, sickness reigns, injustice is the norm and we experience bondage instead of liberty.

Understanding Our Experiences

Understanding that life happens in the midst of this invisible spiritual battle helps us make sense of our lives. Each of us has places in our lives where God's rule has been realized, and we have other places where it has not yet been realized.

If you are a follower of Jesus, God's rule has been realized in your being. Your humanity has been restored to God's design through the death and resurrection of Jesus. God's rule has also been realized through your forgiveness; He has taken care of your sin through the work of His Son.

We each have varying measures of God's rulership in our internal experience. Abiding in the fruit of the Spirit—love, joy, peace and so on—is God's rule over our inner state. Our measure of physical health is correlated to God's rule in our bodies. Our relationships, finances and more all have a design that God lays out in the Scriptures.

In contrast, there are parts of our lives where God's rule has not yet been fully established. While we may have harmony in some relationships, others may be strained. We may experience bondage to a destructive habit or an illness. These are places where the enemy's kingdom is temporarily ruling. This is sometimes referred to as the "already/not-yet" dichotomy of the Kingdom of God. There are places where God's rule has already been established, and there are places where God's rule has not yet been established. We live in the tension of these conditions.

In writing this, I intend no condemnation. We are all progressing toward fullness. God's Kingdom has come into our lives and God's Kingdom is *still* coming into our lives.

Similarly, we can look at our world and see where the Kingdom is already established, and also where it has yet to arrive. Yes, there have been momentous victories: the abolition of the slave trade, the overthrow of despots, the ending of genocides and race wars. Yet there are far more areas to invade: racism, sex trafficking, world poverty and many more. The world cries out for the breakthrough of the Kingdom of God.

Jesus calls us to the battle. He calls us to take the places where God's rule has not yet been established and to work to bring them into alignment with His will. He calls us to go to bed each night leaving the world looking a little more like His design than it was that morning. When we encounter the kingdom of darkness, we cooperate with the Holy Spirit to bring the light.

Some days we will see glorious breakthroughs. Some days we will get to be the very hands and voice of God. We will see God's rule established and the enemy's rule overthrown. It is a glorious and beautiful thing. Other days, we may not win the battle. We will give it our all and advance the cause the best way we know how, but we may not see God's Kingdom come the way we expect. We will not win every battle, but in time we will win the war.

This perspective is vital because it gives us a means to process situations in which we do not see the Kingdom breaking through. We do not have to assign blame; it is not that someone did not have enough faith or that we are lousy Christians. No, the enemy deserves the blame for all his work. The blame stays on him, and we can respond with compassion and kindness to those hurting people who are still looking for Jesus' wholeness to come into their broken lives. The Kingdom paradigm helps us see the world in process. It hinges on more than just our faith. If we experience defeat today, we can accept it and get back to work tomorrow, stronger and wiser.

Jesus has already demonstrated that He is more powerful than Satan's viceroys, Death and the gods of this world. He has broken the powers of darkness, and we know that the eventual victory is guaranteed. The cross proves to us that this is a battle Satan cannot win. Still, he has no intention of going down without a fight. He wants to cause as much havoc as he can while he has the ability.

Meanwhile, we do not get distracted. We do not blame the other soldiers for the fights we do not win, and we do not give up because the battles are hard. Like good soldiers, we stay in the fight and continue to follow the orders from our general, knowing the victory is certain, even if it manifests long after our lifetime on this side of mortality.

Living in this world where God's Kingdom is partially established causes tension. It is far easier to hold to one of these realities than both—either pushing all of God's Kingdom into the future while giving up on seeing it now, or oversimplifying the dynamics of the spiritual battle and believing there is no battle left. This tension means we require patience and perseverance while experiencing dynamic breakthrough.

What Is Happening?

We must be clear on how we think about the places where God's Kingdom has not yet broken in. We can view these places in one of two ways—either as "reality," or as part of God's mysterious ways. How we process this makes all the difference for our experience of faith.

To explore this idea further, let us turn to one of the oldest and most debated topics of faith: the problem of evil. Put simply, the debate is this: *If God is all good and all powerful, why is the world such a mess?* This is a great question and an important reality check on our understanding. It is good to ponder how God rules the universe, but if it is incompatible with our view of reality, we are merely daydreaming about how things could be different.

How we view this issue is absolutely pivotal to our worldview. This topic has likely created more ex-Christians and atheists than any other topic. It is unfortunate, because this need not be the case.

The debate over the problem of evil involves the intersection of two of God's attributes: His goodness and His sovereignty. Both of these attributes are clear in Scripture. God is good, and goodness comes from God. God is also the ultimate sovereign who has the highest authority and rule in the universe. Looking around at the world, however, it is obvious that bad events occur, so what gives?

In framing this question, however, we have assumed definitions of "goodness" and "sovereignty" based on the simplest understanding of each and noting that both are not true in our world.

- **Simple Goodness:** God desires only good things for our lives. His will is never sickness, poverty, sin or death. If it is good, He wants it for us. If it is not good, He does not want it for us.
- **Simple Sovereignty:** As the ultimate sovereign, God gets what He wants all the time. His will always happens.

It is clear that the world of Simple Goodness plus Simple Sovereignty is not the world we live in. The brokenness around us rules out that option. To understand our world, therefore, we have to consider other, more complicated definitions of these characteristics.

- **Complicated Goodness:** God wants goodness in our lives, but His goodness is a long-term game. Things that do not seem good in the short term are actually good in ways that we will someday understand. What looks like evil now will actually cause goodness later, so it is good.

- **Complicated Sovereignty:** God is the ultimate sovereign, but that does not mean His will always happens. He does have ultimate authority, but He does not use that authority to micromanage the universe to ensure that His will always happens. There are other beings, natural and supernatural, that have genuine free will and may resist God's will. As a result, His will does not always happen in the short term, but in the long term, His will shall be established fully.

Now, let us consider the potential options for how God and the universe work and compare them to Scripture. To make this discussion simpler, let us label the three remaining options:

	Simple Sovereignty	Complicated Sovereignty
Simple Goodness	Excluded by problem of evil	Cosmic battle
Complicated Goodness	Cosmic blueprint	Cosmic mystery

As we can see, the problem of evil only excludes one of our potential pictures of the world. What do the other pictures look like? Let us consider each of them from the point of view of living out faith in our daily lives. Suppose event X happens—perhaps a promotion at work, a car accident, the birth of a child or the death of a loved one. How do we process event X in each of these worlds?

Cosmic Mystery

Combine complicated goodness with complicated sovereignty, and you have the cosmic mystery perspective. Here is how it works.

First, we have no way to know whether event X is actually good or evil. While we may like or dislike this event, that is very different from it being good or evil. The latter are descriptions with moral connotations and have nothing to do with personal preference.

Second, with a complicated sovereignty, we cannot know whether event X is from God or not. We do not know whether this event is in alignment with or opposition to God's ultimate authority.

The combination of these two viewpoints means there is no way to know how to handle any given event. Anything that happens in our lives may be good or evil, and it may be from God or not. There are no anchor points from which we can evaluate life. We do not know whether to embrace or resist event X.

This highlights the problem with the cosmic mystery picture of the world. In this view, there is no defined connection point with God. Everything is a mystery; there is nothing to ground our faith. We do not know what God is like or what God is doing in any given event. As a result, we do not understand our role.

This is not only frustrating but also a major theological problem because it undermines one of the major tenets of Christianity: that Jesus came to make God known. "No one has ever seen God; the [Word, Jesus], who is at the Father's side, *he has made him known"* (John 1:18, emphasis added).

God was a great mystery, but He sent His Son so that He could be known. Jesus is the mystery of God revealed. The problem with the cosmic mystery is that this picture negates this revelation and puts God back into the realm of the unknowable. For that reason, we will cross off this picture as one incompatible with the Bible.

Cosmic Blueprint

When we combine complicated goodness with simple sovereignty, this yields the cosmic blueprint perspective.

Unlike the cosmic mystery perspective, the cosmic blueprint perspective does give us a handle to process event X. We are living in a world with simple sovereignty, so whatever event X is, we can be absolutely sure that event X is from God. Event X would not have happened if it was not God's will. Given that event X is God's will, it must be good even though that goodness may only make sense in the long term. At face value, it may appear evil, but eventually, it will be understood as good. With time and a greater perspective, we will understand how event X was necessary.

Given that event X is from God, the only fitting response is to embrace it. Whether it seems good or evil, we will see its goodness in time. In the meantime, we will practice submission and allow the Lord to form us through perseverance and patience. We may not like it. We may wish God's will was different and less painful, but we must make our peace and accept what God has dictated will happen.

Cosmic Battle

We arrive at the cosmic battle perspective by combining simple goodness with complicated sovereignty.

Our handle to process event X through the cosmic battle perspective is different from the cosmic blueprint. In this perspective, because there is a simple goodness, we process event X by identifying it with good or evil. What is good or evil has been revealed biblically in the person and life of Jesus. Everything Jesus stood for and introduced people to is good; the opposite of that is evil. For example, Jesus said, "The thief comes only to steal and kill and destroy" (John 10:10). Thus, in the event of stealing, killing or destroying, we process the source of this event as being from the enemy and therefore view it as an event to be resisted.

With respect to how this plays out in our lives, we find ourselves tasked with a more active role than with the cosmic blueprint perspective. Rather than our faith being about making peace with the will of God that is hard to understand and at times painful, we realize that we factor into God's complicated sovereignty. We have been written into the equation as part of how God rules. We take an active stance, therefore, against events that are discerned as evil, and we take a receptive stance toward events that are discerned as good.[1] In this, we become active participants in the realization of God's will in the universe.

Which World Do We Live In?

Our two potential Christian perspectives, therefore, are the cosmic blueprint and the cosmic battle. Which one defines our world? Which one does the Bible point to?

Many in the Church immediately line up behind the cosmic blueprint perspective. In fact, this is so deeply ingrained in people's thinking that to suggest another perspective is to assert that God is not sovereign—something that could be labeled as heresy.[2] The belief that God's will always happens is a cultural absolute. It comes out in clichés such as "God works in mysterious ways" and "Ours is not to wonder why, ours is but to do and die." Indeed, one need not even be a believer to express the sentiment "Everything happens for a reason."

Of course, the question at hand is not what is popular but what is biblical. What do we see in the Scriptures, and what picture of God does Jesus reveal? Jesus is where our picture of God comes into complete clarity in a way unlike anywhere else—even other parts of Scripture (see John 1:18, Colossians 1:15 or Hebrews 1:1–3 for example).

What picture does Jesus reveal? When I search the Scriptures, I cannot find Jesus living out the cosmic blueprint picture, but He sure seems to live out the cosmic battle picture.

On goodness, Jesus paints a simple picture as we have already seen. He comes only to give abundant life, not to steal, kill and destroy (see John 10:10). When it comes to rulership, Jesus says something very interesting.

> But Jesus called them to him and said, "You know that the rulers of the Gentiles lord it over them, and their great ones exercise authority over them. It shall not be so among you. But whoever would be great among you must be your servant, and whoever would be first among you must be your slave, even as the Son of Man came not to be served but to serve, and to give his life as a ransom for many."
>
> Matthew 20:25–28

Jesus points out that the rulers of the Gentiles inflict their authority upon others. They rule by forcing their will to happen. They tell people to stop doing certain things and start doing other things. They try to get their will executed all the time. Jesus makes a point of saying that this is *not* the Kingdom way because that is not how He operates. He is not here to exercise top-down rulership but to lay down His life and serve. It is fascinating to me that much of the Church thinks that God is exercising exactly the kind of top-down rulership in the universe that Jesus eschews.

Further, when we see Jesus interacting with people, I do not see a "submission-is-the-only-option" posture. He never tells someone their sickness or demonization is from God; instead, He resists these things and overthrows them. When He comes up against something that He discerns is evil, Jesus does not put up with it. He fights back. Remember, the reason the Son of God came was to destroy the works of the devil (see 1 John 3:8). Jesus makes it clear that our world is not the cosmic blueprint. It is the cosmic battle.

One last point on the distinction between these two perspectives: I cannot find any way to make Kingdom theology fit the cosmic blueprint perspective. By definition, the cosmic blueprint perspective presents only one kingdom, not two.

Sometimes people attempt to fit these two together. They try to fit together the sovereignty delineated by the cosmic blueprint with the concept of two kingdoms at war. They want to believe both Kingdom theology and Calvinism. Yet the biblical definition of "kingdom" excludes this thinking. Remember, a kingdom is not a nation, it is a rule—the expression of a will (see Matthew 6:10). If a kingdom were a nation, then it would be possible to have a nation of good and a nation of evil with God's will overseeing how these two nations battle it out. That is a consistent picture; it just does not use "kingdom" in the way the Bible does.

In the cosmic blueprint perspective, there are two nations but only one rule—God's rule. Hence, God's will always determines events. We might pretend the enemy has a rule, but in the cosmic blueprint perspective, Satan and his henchmen are just puppets in God's great cosmic machine. Satan, therefore, has no independent acting power. That lack of acting power excludes a reign, as the Scriptures define "kingdom."

If, on the other hand, there are indeed two kingdoms—two wills in conflict—that means our world is caught up in a cosmic battle.

What Does This Mean?

For many of us, the cosmic battle is a new perspective that takes some getting used to. We have been handed the cosmic blueprint perspective from before we were even saved. If we now accept the cosmic battle perspective, it means we have to rethink how we process life. That is a momentous shift.

I want to conclude this chapter with a few important ramifications of the cosmic battle perspective.

Revealed Good/Evil

A major adjustment arising from the difference in perspectives is the requirement to discern whether or not something is from God. In the cosmic blueprint perspective, everything is to be unquestionably accepted—no discernment is required. In the cosmic battle perspective, however, we are called to discernment. Some things are from the Lord and are to be accepted; other things are from the enemy and are to be resisted. This ability to exercise discernment is actually a sign of maturity. "But solid food is for the mature, for those who have their powers of discernment trained by constant practice to distinguish good from evil" (Hebrews 5:14).

How do we grow in this discernment? The Word of God is our standard. We look to what has already been demonstrated by Jesus as good and evil. If Jesus would see it as evil, so should we. If Jesus would see it as good, we would do well to do the same.

Our Assignment

Another adjustment involves taking a more active posture in our faith. The cosmic blueprint puts our faith in a passive posture, making it our job to accept, not act. In the cosmic battle, however, we recognize that God has made us part of the solution. We have been drafted into the Lord's work, and it is a good soldier who engages the enemy when he or she recognizes it. "And I assign to you, as my Father assigned to me, a kingdom" (Luke 22:29).

Of course, this viewpoint can become legalistic and unhealthy if taken to extremes. My point is that, in general, our faith should assume an active stance. If we cannot point to places where we have recently worked to dislodge the kingdom of darkness, that is a problem to be resolved.

Prayer Is Not about Yes/No/Wait

A common element of the cosmic blueprint perspective is the idea that prayer is largely a minimally engaged activity. We throw up a prayer to God and wait on His divine will to take it from there. I commonly hear this phrased as, "Every prayer is answered; it's *yes, no* or *wait*. Our job is to pray and be content with whatever answer God sends our way."

The problem with this approach is that the Bible reveals a completely different concept of prayer. In the Scriptures, prayer is about engaging spiritual dynamics to release God's will. This is why we see examples of prayer engaged with spiritual warfare (see Daniel 10:12–14) and why Jesus teaches that we must persist in prayer and not give up (see Luke 11:5–13; 18:1–8).

When God's Kingdom Does Not Come

How should we understand circumstances in which God's rule is not fully established? We can view them as a part of the battlefield that God is still working to win. We know that God's will is established perfectly in heaven (see Matthew 6:10), but between now and then, the world is a spiritual battlefield. We further understand that the reality of God's Kingdom is merely a breath away. God's Kingdom is available and present; it is active on our earth, breaking in and releasing a new creation to supplant the old one.

Simultaneously, we understand the reality of the Kingdom battle, and when that reality presents itself in the form of God's will not yet realized, we can acknowledge that fact without casting blame. God's Kingdom is already active on the earth, but it is not present in every situation. Not yet. The Kingdom is still advancing on the earth.

God Is Still Working

Accepting that God's sovereignty means not everything that happens is His will can be difficult at first. What is left? Two things specifically.

First, while everything has not been redeemed now, everything will be redeemed eventually. Whether or not we see that redemption in this life, we know the redemption is coming.

Second, we know that God is working toward that redemption in every situation, whether He was the cause or not. Not everything is *from* God, but that does not mean God's hands are tied from working in any situation. In fact, Scripture makes it clear that even if events originate with the enemy, God is able to turn them to His purposes. "And we know that for those who love God all things work together for good, for those who are called according to his purpose" (Romans 8:28).

Not all things are from God, but for people moving toward God's Kingdom—those who love Him and are called by Him—God is present in all things and working toward the good. This means there is no situation in which God is not at work; therefore, we can partner with Him to release His Kingdom. No situation is so dark and evil that it excludes God from redeeming it.

We Hang Together Regardless

In our journey of faith, we can expect to experience Kingdom breakthroughs both now and eventually. In both experiences, we are called to love, support and walk with our brothers and sisters. "Rejoice with those who rejoice, weep with those who weep" (Romans 12:15).

It can be difficult to embrace both situations. It is much easier in some ways to hold on to one and let go of the other. To relieve the tension, we can easily let go of any expectation of God's Kingdom breaking through and establishing His will. When we hit major disappointments, it can be a relief to just write the whole thing off rather than maintain hope. On the other side, I have also seen people disconnect from others in need when the Kingdom does not break in. They do not want to admit that things did not work, so they cut off any contact with those they were trying to help. That is not the compassionate way of kindness that Jesus calls us to. We are called to journey with our brothers and sisters to the mountaintops and through the valleys.

We Can Trust God; He Is Safe

Another drawback to the cosmic blueprint perspective is that it frames God as emotionally threatening. Sure, God is "good" somehow, but it is hard to trust God when His goodness gives me cancer. It is hard to feel safe when God is causing (or allowing) epidemics, sex trafficking, genocide and more. The idea that God uses a lot of things that appear evil can easily develop into fear. *When is that evil-feeling-goodness going to come my way?* It is hard to feel loved by a father who you are constantly worrying will hurt you. You may take some solace in the fact that you know it is God who is doing it, but trust is difficult with someone who seems to have such a painful track record.

In the cosmic battle perspective, God is emotionally safe. He is not causing horrible things; you do not need to be worried about Him dispatching evil into your life. Furthermore, while you are not guaranteed that evil will never afflict your life, you are guaranteed that if it does, God will be there with you. There

93

is no such thing as a pain-free life. The promise is that He will be your comforter and will walk with you in the midst of everything.

The Kingdom calls us into a messy world—a world in process, one experiencing a battle for redemption. Jesus has come and launched the effort, but now He looks to us to partner with Him in the ongoing task. He will be with us along the way. We will find that in the midst of the battle, it is His goodness that refreshes us. The battle is real, but we never face it alone. Instead, like David, we can learn to commune with the Lord in the midst of the battle.

> Even though I walk through the valley of the shadow of death, I will fear no evil, for you are with me; your rod and your staff, they comfort me. You prepare a table before me in the presence of my enemies; you anoint my head with oil; my cup overflows.
>
> Psalm 23:4–5

To understand how we participate in that battle, we must fight the way Jesus fought. The Holy Spirit is critical in that process. He is the one who releases the inbreaking of the Kingdom. He is the subject we turn to in the next chapter.

IMPACT POINTS

- Kingdom theology implies that God's goodness is simple and His sovereignty is complicated.
- God will ultimately have the complete victory, but His will does not always happen during our immediate circumstances.
- We are actively involved in the Kingdom confrontation. God's will is tied to our involvement. Our stance as believers should be active, not passive, when it comes to God's will in our world.

THE SPIRIT AND KINGDOM

I HAVE ALWAYS FOUND myself inspired by Steve Jobs. Maybe I have been drinking the Apple Kool-Aid, but I find his role as a creative visionary deeply compelling.[1] Steve Jobs and his friend Steve Wozniak founded Apple Computer in their twenties, working in Jobs' father's garage. By the time Jobs passed away 35 years later, he was running the most valuable company in the world. Steve was far from a perfect human being; indeed, his flaws were as evident as his genius, but no one can argue that his was a remarkable accomplishment.

Along the way, Jobs disrupted industry after industry, reinventing the way the world worked in the modern digital revolution. He demonstrated a sense of prescience—an ability to see where things were headed and get there first. It is generally recognized that over the course of his career, he transformed six industries: personal computers, animated movies, music, phones, tablet computing and digital publishing. We might even add that he breathed fresh life into retailing as well. It was this ability to peer into the future and bring it into the present that infused his company with life and made him one of the most successful businesspersons of all time.

Apple's repeated ability to create the future has infused the company with an epic sense of energy and vision. Apple does not seem to have customers as much as raving fans. Tickets to Apple's product launches are craved more than most high-profile rock concerts, and some of Apple's commercials are so powerful that I cannot make it through them without tearing up. (Just tried again with "Here's to the Crazy Ones." Nope, still cannot make it.)

In a way that far exceeds Steve Jobs, Jesus is bringing His creative power into our world, disrupting this present reality with His new creation. His revolution is not digital, it is spiritual—a revolution aimed at the fundamental core of things, seeking to restore all the broken things in the world back to their original design. Jobs may have had the ability to *peer* into the future, but Jesus *owns* the future. His future is crashing into our present and disrupting it far more than Apple ever will.

The Kingdom Unleashed

How does Jesus' future crash into our present? Furthermore, how do we join in that process? We do not have the ability to force it to happen of our own volition. It is only in partnership with the Holy Spirit that we can release into this present reality the power of the age to come.

Even Jesus partnered with the Spirit to release God's Kingdom. In John 5, we see a fascinating verse. Jesus has just healed a man, and as usual, the Pharisees are upset because Jesus healed him on the Sabbath. In the ensuing argument, Jesus simply replies that He could only heal because God was working on the Sabbath to release healing. In the midst of that, Jesus adds something revealing. "So Jesus said to them, 'Truly, truly, I say to you, the Son can do nothing of his own accord, but only what he sees the Father doing. For whatever the Father does, that the Son does likewise'" (John 5:19).

This shocks me. Jesus says He *cannot* do things like this outside of partnership with the Father. Only in cooperation with the Father can Jesus release healing.

Let us take a closer look at this. There is a pattern that God uses to release His power into the world. We find it in the first verses of the Bible where God creates the world itself. "The earth was without form and void, and darkness was over the face of the deep. And the Spirit of God was hovering over the face of the waters. And God said, 'Let there be light,' and there was light" (Genesis 1:2–3).

In this scene, the earth is chaotic and shapeless; it is not conforming to the design of the Father. The Holy Spirit hovers over the chaos, and God speaks His Word into that hovering presence. It is not just God's Word but the Word and the Spirit partnering together in the process of Creation. The Word and the Spirit together unleash the creative power of God to form a new reality.

When Jesus comes to earth, the Word becomes flesh (see John 1:14). The Word takes up residence in a human being and walks the earth. It is at Jesus' baptism, though, that another layer gets added as the Spirit comes to rest upon Him (see Matthew 3:16–17). The hovering presence of the Spirit joins with the Word, and God's power is released to create new realities just as it was at creation. This is why we see Jesus thrust into miraculous ministry after His baptism. From here, the Spirit drives Jesus into the wilderness, from which He returns in "the power of the Spirit" (Luke 4:14) and delivers His ministry's mission statement:

> The Spirit of the Lord is upon me, because he has anointed me to proclaim good news to the poor. He has sent me to proclaim liberty to the captives and recovering of sight to the blind, to set at liberty those who are oppressed, to proclaim the year of the Lord's favor.
>
> Luke 4:18–19

Because the Spirit of the Lord is upon Him, Jesus is anointed to proclaim the good news and work miracles. It is the joining of the Word and the Spirit that unleashes the power of God and enacts God's rule on earth. When the Word and the Spirit collide, the Kingdom is released.

Passing the Baton

Jesus commissions His disciples to continue the work of unleashing the Kingdom. This is the core of the great commission. Satan's former authority has now been obtained by Jesus, and we are sent out under that authority (see Matthew 28:18–20).

This authority is not something we carry in ourselves; rather, it is something we broker on behalf of our King Jesus. We are sent out to extend Jesus' authority in places where He is not physically present.

Consider the story of the centurion in Matthew 8. When Jesus offers to come and heal his servant, the centurion replies that he is not worthy for Jesus to come. He says it is not necessary anyway because he understands how authority works. "For I too am a man under authority, with soldiers under me. And I say to one, 'Go,' and he goes, and to another, 'Come,' and he comes, and to my servant, 'Do this,' and he does it" (Matthew 8:9).

There is authority above him and there are soldiers and servants below him. As a link in the chain of authority, his words do not just represent himself; they are words that have been sanctioned by the authority above him. He does not merely speak to his soldiers as a centurion; he speaks on behalf of the general who has placed him under his authority.

The centurion believes it is not necessary for Jesus to come to his house. He realizes that Jesus is also a man under authority, here on earth under the authority of the Father. As such, He represents God to sickness and malady. Jesus' words are not just His words, they are the Father's words, and the centurion believes the Father can heal with a simple word.

This idea of authority stretching through the representative runs through much of Jesus' teaching. When He sends the disciples out, He says, "Whoever receives you receives me, and whoever receives me receives him who sent me" (Matthew 10:40).

This is how Jesus sends us out today. He is atop the chain of authority; all authority in heaven and on earth has been given to Him. Now we go under that authority, extending Jesus' authority through our lives to the world around us. We become the middle link in the authority chain, representing our King to the rest of creation.

This is why we pray in Jesus' name. "In Jesus' name" is not a magic phrase to be attached to the end of a prayer so that God will hear it. Praying something and attaching "in Jesus' name" does not mean we are praying in Jesus' name. To pray in Jesus' name is to pray on Jesus' behalf. This is what we see in applications throughout the New Testament (see Mark 9:38; Luke 10:17; Acts 9:34; Acts 16:16–18).

The Mandated Kingdom

Most people find this message both liberating and challenging. *Wow! I'm sent as Jesus' representative to step in on His behalf and extend His authority through my life. Amazing! Oh, but that means I should be able to point to God moving through my life, or I'm not walking out the great commission.*

Yes, it is an incredible message, but in the haunting words of the recent Spider-Man movies, "With great power comes great responsibility." The message of the Kingdom confronts us with a higher level of responsibility than we may have realized. There is no room for passive Christianity in this message. It requires us to take seriously the ministry of the Holy Spirit. I know this firsthand. For much of my life, I felt that learning to cooperate with the Holy Spirit to release charismatic gifts was an optional pursuit—something for radical Christians. At best, it was icing on the cake. The real pursuit was to preach the Gospel of salvation . . . or so I thought.

Now, please do not misunderstand me. I am one hundred percent for preaching salvation. I preach the Gospel of salvation more than most. I thoroughly believe in the salvation Gospel and have experienced it setting me free in ways I never even imagined. That being said, I think we need to take seriously Jesus' words to the disciples as He returned to heaven. "But you will receive power when the Holy Spirit has come upon you, and you will be my witnesses in Jerusalem and in all Judea and Samaria, and to the end of the earth" (Acts 1:8). There is more to the Gospel than salvation.

Consider this: Jesus is speaking to the group of people who have lived with Him for three years. These are people who are much more qualified to preach the Gospel than you or I will ever be. They know the message. Yet Jesus tells them to stay put because, to be the kind of witnesses He wants them to be, they need to receive power from the Spirit. According to Jesus, it is not just about witnessing to a message—the disciples were already eminently qualified for that—but rather about bearing witness to a new *reality*, one that requires the power of the Spirit.

For too long, the Church has made optional what Jesus made mandatory. Jesus never indicated that the power of the Holy Spirit is for those who are interested; it is a requirement for all, because without the Holy Spirit, it is impossible to release the Kingdom.

There is a difference between pursuing the *fruit* of the Kingdom and releasing the Kingdom itself. We know that when God's rule is fully realized, there will be no poverty, sickness, injustice or hatred. There is a difference, however, between pursuing the Kingdom on our own and participating in the ruling activity of God. The message of the Kingdom is that *God's rule* will abolish these things. The message is *not* that if *we* abolish these things, we will have established God's rule. God's plan is that the means of the Kingdom—the inbreaking power of the age to come—will accomplish these ends of the Kingdom.

At times, I wonder how much we may try to achieve the ends of the Kingdom without the means of the Kingdom. It is not always obvious that we cannot solve these problems ourselves. For example, is it really necessary to look for the power of the Spirit to care for the poor? Can we not just get organized and use our resources effectively?

Again, I am all for effective resource allocation, and I do believe that we should use what we already have at our disposal. Yet I do not believe we can neglect the power of the Kingdom, because as we have seen, these structural issues of society have spiritual powers behind them. We may be able to redistribute resources, but that is not the full solution. That is treating the symptoms of a spiritual condition driving lack in our world. To fully resolve humankind's problems, we need *both* resource allocation to meet present needs and the power of the Spirit to deal with root causes.

Consider how the early Church confronted this issue of injustice:

Now in these days when the disciples were increasing in number, a complaint by the Hellenists arose against the Hebrews because their widows were being neglected in the daily distribution. And the twelve summoned the full number of the disciples and said, "It is not right that we should give up preaching the word of God to serve tables. Therefore, brothers, pick out from among you seven

men of good repute, full of the Spirit and of wisdom, whom we
will appoint to this duty."

Acts 6:1–3

Notice what they looked for: individuals who were full of the
Spirit and wisdom. The requirements were spiritual power and
the ability to create natural solutions. The early Church knew
they needed both, because they needed people who would con-
struct both natural and spiritual solutions to a problem that was
both natural and spiritual in nature. If we want to be effective
in bringing God's Kingdom rule to our society, we will do well
to pursue it with the combination of natural wisdom and the
power of the Spirit.

My experience is that the Holy Spirit really does have the solutions to these social issues. When Peter quotes Joel 2 on the Day
of Pentecost, he clearly implies the dissolution of racial, gender
and age barriers. The Spirit has the power to unite people's hearts
like nothing else can.

Five years ago, we started thinking carefully about the ethnic
diversity in our church. Our church was planted forty years earlier
and had grown as most church plants do—through social net-
works connected to the founding couples. While organic growth
was a good thing, an unintended side effect was that, while our
community has a relatively high degree of racial diversity, our
church was overwhelmingly Caucasian.

Recently, however, we noticed something incredible. Our
church's ethnic composition was now within one percent of
our community's demographics. It was a great moment. As we
looked back at what had brought us there, the overwhelming
factor was the manifest presence of the Holy Spirit. Of course,
we took intentional steps to partner with what God was doing
in other places, but the predominant driver has been the fact

that when the Spirit moves, He gathers all peoples together. In places where we have cultivated God's presence and power, this produced not only a higher degree of diversity but a more loving diversity. God has drawn us together in ways that we could not have achieved on our own.

I understand that it is not always exciting to consider our responsibility to learn to move in the power of the Spirit. Indeed, it can be sobering. Remember my story, however. I disdained this stuff for years. I saw all the abuses and strange practices. Frankly, some of it was weird. Why could we not just stick to "normal" Christianity?

That was exactly what I thought. What I had forgotten is that no part of our faith is normal. Think about it:

- We believe that God was born as a human being to a virgin. What is normal about that?
- We believe that God decided to hang out and do carpentry for thirty years before He started acting at all like God.
- We believe that God getting beat up and killed but then "Oh, not really" is somehow the solution to the world's problems.
- We believe that God wrote a book but that He used other people, not His Son, to write about His Son.
- We believe that we have been born spiritually a second time and that someday we will get brand-new bodies.

What is not weird about this list? How is being empowered by the Spirit of God and releasing the power of the Kingdom any stranger than what is already on this list? The fact is, it is all weird; we are just more used to some of it than to other parts.

I understand that all of this stuff can be weird. It can seem "out there" and something we would rather leave behind. That is not an option, however, because Jesus is Lord. We are not Lord. We have surrendered our will to His, and Jesus beckons each of His disciples to come follow Him. We are called to do what He did, the way He did it. Jesus was empowered by the Spirit to release the Kingdom, and obedience requires that we do likewise.

Learning to Walk in Power

How do we walk in that power today? What does it look like for us to release into our world the powers of the age to come? The Father's plan is to use the same dynamic with us that He did with Jesus. We now get to participate in bringing the Word and Spirit together. Releasing the Kingdom is indeed the birthright of those who believe. The prerequisite qualification is the new birth. "Jesus answered him, 'Truly, truly, I say to you, unless one is born again he cannot see the kingdom of God'" (John 3:3).

Why is the new birth important? Because in the new birth, Christ takes up residence in our hearts through faith (see Ephesians 3:17). The Word comes and dwells within us and is accessed by faith. When we speak from faith, the Word within us is released through our words. "But what does it say? 'The word is near you, in your mouth and in your heart' (that is, the word of faith that we proclaim)" (Romans 10:8).

It is ours to both *believe* that Christ dwells in us and to *speak* from the faith that He really is in us, that His power flows through us and that His will is to release the Kingdom. Our job is to connect with the reality of the Kingdom and live from that place.

At the same time, our faith declarations are not the entire equation. If we fail to understand this, we could end up trying to force things to happen through our proclamations alone. The power is not in our faith; the power is in God—His Word and Spirit. Faith is the bridge that releases the Word through us.

The joining of God's Word and Spirit releases God's rule into any situation. Speaking the Word in faith is part of the process, but it must be the Word spoken into the hovering presence of the Spirit to catalyze a new reality. For us to learn to do the works of the Kingdom, we must learn how to speak in faith when we see what the Father is doing. We need to grow in discernment and our ability to perceive the Spirit of God hovering over the chaos in someone's life. Then we can step in and partner with the person by adding our words in faith.

In 1 Corinthians 12, Paul writes an entire chapter on the dynamics of the spirit realm and partnering with God. The church in Corinth is very active in spiritual things, so Paul offers clarification on how to partner with the Lord. He begins with something important (something I missed for a long time): "Now there are varieties of gifts, but the same Spirit; and there are varieties of service, but the same Lord; and there are varieties of activities, but it is the same God who empowers them all in everyone" (1 Corinthians 12:4–6).

Paul sets up three different categories of spiritual activity: gifts, service and activities. Each of these is a direct interaction with a different member of the Godhead. The verses that follow explore each of these categories in more depth.[2] Paul then turns to discuss the gifts of the Spirit. "To each is given the manifestation of the Spirit for the common good" (1 Corinthians 12:7).

Catching Paul's intent here, this category includes "manifestations of the Spirit." These are ways the Holy Spirit shows up. Knowing these, we can perceive the hovering presence of God as He draws near the chaos in someone's life. These manifestations are not gifts that we have; the gift is the Holy Spirit. The Holy Spirit has the ability to manifest in many ways, though, so we must learn to look for the way He is presently manifesting. When He does, He is working to benefit someone.

A common way that some understand the gifts of the Spirit is to think of them as things with which we are born. God chooses to give us gifts of words of wisdom, faith or interpretation of tongues, for example. From that point on, our job is to learn to discern which gifts we have and serve faithfully with them. I do think there are gifts that work that way, but that is not the accurate picture for the gifts of the Spirit. The service and activities listed in these verses work in the picture described above; only some are accessible to us, and it is our job to discern what we have and faithfully serve with them. People often confuse these three categories and argue from the list of activities empowered by God that they cannot act in certain manifestations of the Spirit (see 1 Corinthians 12:28–30).

This logic misses Paul's point entirely. This is a different gift that functions differently. God does appoint certain roles that are not for everyone. That list includes prophet, miracle worker, healer, tongues speaker and interpreter. These appointments, though, are a separate discussion from what Paul is discussing earlier when he is talking about the manifestations of the Spirit. This was the point of Paul's introduction in 1 Corinthians 12:4–6.

While not every believer is a prophet, every believer can partner with the Spirit when He manifests as a prophecy. Not everyone is called to an appointment of a healer, but everyone can partner with the Spirit when He is releasing a gift of healing. The Spirit's presence upon us all is the sign of the new world. We know we are people of the future because the Spirit has been poured out upon us. It is not because we have *spiritual gifts*, but because we have *the Spirit*.

Kingdom Breakthrough for the Rest of Us

To release the Kingdom, we must learn two things: how to discern the Spirit of God as He hovers over creation, and how to speak in faith so the Word and Spirit come together in power. As we learn to do these, we will see incredible things happen.

I spend a lot of time training people to do the things I am discussing here. In my experience, most of us believe that releasing the Kingdom is about special gifting or unusually anointed people. It is not. A long time ago, I gave up trying to be gifted or anointed. The gifts belong to the Spirit; they are His and not mine. There is one anointed One, and He already lives in me. The Kingdom is not about me—it is about God. It is not about what I have or do not have; it is about what He has and what He gives.

At times, it can *feel* as if you do not have the gifts you need to minister. This can be because you are looking to your own abilities. Actually, you can minister, you just do not know how to cooperate with God in that specific way yet. The good news is that you can learn to recognize when the Holy Spirit manifests as a word of knowledge, a healing, a tongue, a prophecy or a discerning of spirits. For some people, it comes quicker or easier than for others; these are the ones we label as "gifted."

Whether it feels natural to you or not, you can learn. I have seen too many people learn how to do these things to believe anyone is hopeless. I have worked with thousands of people all over the globe to help them understand how to recognize when the Spirit manifests in various ways. It works the same every time. People are skeptical at first, then hopeful, then shocked as it starts working. Finally, they are astounded as they begin to prophesy, heal the sick or cast out demons.

The ministry of the Spirit is not random, even though many think it is. When they pray for healing, they are essentially throwing dice. *Maybe it will work, maybe not.* I do not believe in the slightest that it is random. Jesus did not release the Kingdom that way. I do not see Him praying, hoping it is going to work this time. In fact, He got frustrated with His disciples when they could not cast out a demon and heal a mute, epileptic boy (see Mark

9:14–29). The wind of the Spirit blows where He wishes, but we are to learn to flow along with Him. "The wind blows where it wishes, and you hear its sound, but you do not know where it comes from or where it goes. So it is with everyone who is born of the Spirit" (John 3:8).

If we do not learn to flow with the Spirit, then releasing the Kingdom will feel random. We will give it our best shot, and if we get lucky, we will happen to bump into the Holy Spirit. On the other hand, as we learn to attune to Him, staying completely in harmony with Him, knowing where He is hovering and moving where He moves, we will experience what we see in the Scriptures. Time and time again, we see the disciples detecting the hovering presence of the Spirit and releasing the power of the future age into their present world.

> Now at Lystra there was a man sitting who could not use his feet. He was crippled from birth and had never walked. He listened to Paul speaking. And Paul, looking intently at him and seeing that he had faith to be made well, said in a loud voice, "Stand upright on your feet." And he sprang up and began walking.
>
> Acts 14:8–10

> Seeing Peter and John about to go into the temple, he asked to receive alms. And Peter directed his gaze at him, as did John, and said, "Look at us." And he fixed his attention on them, expecting to receive something from them. But Peter said, "I have no silver and gold, but what I do have I give to you. In the name of Jesus Christ of Nazareth, rise up and walk!" And he took him by the right hand and raised him up, and immediately his feet and ankles were made strong.
>
> Acts 3:3–7

What would it be like to partner regularly with the Spirit in releasing the Kingdom of God? It might look like this. You perceive the Spirit of God hovering over people just as Peter and John did, so you step in and release the Kingdom of God. You see the Holy Spirit release a prophetic word to a co-worker, so you chat with him for five minutes and release something life-changing into his life. You see the Holy Spirit hovering over your neighbor who is complaining of a migraine, so you release the Kingdom of God over your backyard fence and the migraine lifts. You are talking with your cousin whose marriage is failing and you sense the Spirit releasing words of wisdom and faith, so you step in and share not just your best thoughts but God's powerful words into her situation.

My good friend Brian Blount is one of the people I know who exemplifies these qualities well. He is firmly committed to releasing the Kingdom of God as he goes through his everyday life. As he does, he keeps his heart open to sense what God is doing, and then he steps in and responds. Brian Blount tells this story of a Kingdom adventure he and two friends had in a taxi with a driver who was a devout Muslim.[3]

As we talked, I asked [our driver] about her family and about her faith.

I purposefully did not say anything to her about me being a Christian or about Jesus—I just listened to her story.

A little while into the conversation, I felt I had four words of knowledge about [her] health—stress headaches, difficulty sleeping, and pain in her lower back and neck.

I asked her if she had these problems. "Yes, I have all of those," she replied in shock. I asked her what her pain level was now on a scale of 1–10, and she said it was a 9. "How did you know this? I've had this pain for 4 years."

I told her I have a gift where I get pictures and impressions of what is going on in people's lives. "Wow, that is very interesting," she replied.

"Would you like me to do something about those conditions and take the pain away?"

"You can do that? How?"

"Yes, I can. When you drop me off, if you give me one minute, I can take care of it." She asked me how I would take care of it, and I explained that I would just speak to her pain and tell it to go, and it will. "Please do," she said, still perplexed.

We continued talking, and about three minutes later, [she] blurted out, "Did you just do that thing?" I told her I had not done anything. "I'm hot all over my body!" she said. "Like I'm sweating. And all the pain just left my back!"

"Well, that's very interesting," I said with a smile. [My friends] were in the back seat trying to hide their shock as well. The Holy Spirit was sovereignly healing her. [She] went on to explain that her back pain was totally gone, and her neck was very hot as well, and the pain in her neck had gone down to a level four. She was bewildered.

As we continued to talk, [our driver] asked me for my phone number. "I would like to stay in contact with you," she said. When we arrived at the memorial, I asked [her] if the rest of the pain had left. "No, but I'm still hot all over."

I told her the rest of the pain would leave now. I asked if I could touch her hand, and I was surprised when she said yes because I knew this was not something a Muslim woman would normally allow. I commanded all the remaining neck pain to leave. I prayed twice, and the second time, all the pain left.

[She] asked me how I had done that. I explained, "The gift I have is the Holy Spirit. I'm a Christian. What you just experienced was Jesus healing you. Jesus loves you. . . . Have you ever experienced Allah like this or received healing from Allah?" She replied no. "Well, this is what Jesus does, and I'm a follower of Jesus. As Christians, this is what we do. This is what Jesus does. This is the love of God expressed to you, that Jesus is pursuing a relationship with you."

At the end of the conversation, [she] said, "I believe in Allah, but I do not know how you did this." Again, I told her that Jesus was the one who did this. She was definitely perplexed and having to rethink a lot of what she believed about Jesus. At about that time we had to get going because the security guards around the memorial were preventing cars from lingering.

Brian is not a hero; he is just available. He is intentionally available, and God uses him to touch people with healing, salvation, freedom and love as he lives his everyday life. He prays for telemarketers on the phone and drive-through workers at McDonald's. He puts into practice what we can all learn: to look for opportunities to cooperate with the Holy Spirit and release the Kingdom of God.

To learn this, we will need to take a deeper look at how to recognize and step in when the Holy Spirit hovers over someone's life. That is the task for our next chapter.

IMPACT POINTS

- The Kingdom of God is released when the Word and the Spirit come together. This pattern is woven through Scripture.
- The Word of God now dwells in the hearts of believers through faith, so our job is to identify the hovering presence of the Spirit and speak words by faith to release the Kingdom.
- What are usually thought of as "gifts of the Spirit" are the different ways the Holy Spirit hovers over the chaos in people's lives. The gifts belong to Him, not us, so they are all available for us to learn to step into.

PARTNERING WITH GOD TODAY

AS A YOUNG BOY, I fell in love with the night sky. I remember looking up and seeing the stars and thinking: *Wow! Each one of these is a whole solar system all by itself!* The sense of wonder and awe was palpable. My heart leapt for joy, imagining a lifetime of discovery to know even a sliver of it.

Nature has a way of leaving us awestruck, right? Whether it is the majesty of a mountain range, the beautiful tapestry of the sunset, the vastness of the ocean or the wonder of the night sky, we can find ourselves connecting with a world so much larger than our lives that we get swept up in the *beyondness* of it all.

It was this boyish delight at uncovering the world around me that eventually guided me into the sciences. To discover something new thrilled me and left me hungering for more. There was no end game; it was learning for the sheer joy of experiencing it.

Growing up, the Holy Spirit seemed like a total mystery, but instead of filling me with wonder, He unsettled me. I understood that somehow He was God, but it confused me. Jesus, on the other hand, made sense to me. Jesus represented God the Father, but what was the deal with the Holy Spirit? He was kind of a missing third member of the Trinity, or perhaps the third wheel with the Father and Son. I knew He was God or something, but I did not realize how all that worked.

At the time, I wondered if that was somehow a product of His old-sounding name: The Holy *Ghost*. Jesus I could get because He was . . . well . . . a person. But a ghost? How was I supposed to make sense of that? He sounded spooky. Weird. Unsettling.

While I do not think referring to Him as a ghost helps, in hindsight, I see my concern and confusion had more to do with not understanding how He fit into the story of faith. I knew that Jesus was the one who did all the work to save me, and the Father was the one with whom Jesus restored me to relationship, but how was the Holy Spirit involved? Without a clear understanding of how I could expect Him to be a part of my faith journey, He felt shrouded in mystery.

The Holy Spirit is indeed God, every bit as much as the Father and the Son. In fact, in some ways He is the easiest to get to know because He is constantly active around us and working to intersect our lives. When we understand the story of the Kingdom of God, we recognize why the Holy Spirit is critical and how we should expect to know Him. Everything in the Kingdom comes from the Father—He is the one who has set the original design that is being released again into the world. Everything in the Kingdom is available because of Jesus. He came as the conquering King of the Kingdom and anchored that Kingdom to our world through His overthrow of Satan. But everything in the Kingdom comes to us through the Holy Spirit. The Spirit of God is the one who is landing the Kingdom on earth today by inviting us into partnership with Him.

If your journey is like mine, you will need to spend some time to actually get to know the Holy Spirit. The Holy Spirit is not an *it*. He is a *he*. He is a person. He has a personality. He talks. He has preferences. He walks with us through life. It is in coming to know the Holy Spirit that we are fruitful in ministry. God is supremely relational. His goal is to walk with us.

This is so important. At times, I see people who are looking for a formula. "What do I need to do to release the Kingdom? How do I see people healed and delivered, break down racism, fight poverty?" God does not give us a formula. He gives us Himself and ensures that we will have everything we need through relationship with Him.

> When the Spirit of truth comes, he will guide you into all the truth, for he will not speak on his own authority, but whatever he hears he will speak, and he will declare to you the things that are to come. He will glorify me, for he will take what is mine and declare it to you. All that the Father has is mine; therefore I said that he will take what is mine and declare it to you.
>
> John 16:13–15

The formula for effectively releasing the Kingdom is this: Partner with God in the present moment. We do not have the ability to create the Kingdom. We cannot force the Kingdom to intersect with this world, but we can partner with what we see God initiating. God is always at work (see John 5:17), so we get to learn more and more how to recognize our divine partner and cooperate with whatever He is up to.

Life becomes more fun as we get curious about what God is presently doing. As I have grown, the Holy Spirit has become a lot less mysterious, in some ways—yet the more I get to know Him, the more I realize I am rarely tracking with Him. I now know what He is like, but rarely do I feel that I can know what He is going to do next. As I have come to know Him better, my view of Him has changed from a disconcerting figure to an ever-new friend.

In this chapter, we will unpack some specifics of how to partner with the Holy Spirit. While I hope this is helpful, I have found that nothing can replace the hands-on experience of being discipled by someone who knows how to flow with the Spirit and equip others to do the same. This is why we started the School of Kingdom Ministry, a training program that any church can host to effectively release people in the kinds of things we are discussing here. Consider this chapter a brief introduction. There is much, much more in that resource.

Getting Started

So how do we operate in partnership with the Holy Spirit? We want to be people who live out the Kingdom in practice. How do we get there?

The biblical starting point is an experience called being *filled with the Spirit*. We repeatedly see this as a key experience for a believer on his or her journey to effectively ministering the Kingdom (see Acts 2:1–4; 4:8; 4:31; 13:9). We see intentionality to have believers filled with the Spirit if they have not had that experience (see Acts 19:1–6), and we are instructed to repeatedly be filled with the Spirit to avoid foolishness and excess (see Ephesians 5:18).

The issue of being filled with the Spirit is one that has caused much division and dissension within the Body of Christ. I find this most unfortunate. Thinking carefully about our terminology can help us avoid common pitfalls.

Let me begin by saying that I do not believe it is helpful to think in terms of first- or second-class believers—the distinction being people who have or have not been filled with the Spirit. While it is clear the infilling is biblical and is linked to empowering for ministry, the goal is certainly not to create tiers of believers.

It is important to specify how we mean "filled." We commonly contrast "filled" with "empty," and that can easily lead to a stratifying of believers: those who have received the Spirit and those who have not. Tiered thinking becomes the inevitable consequence, which is nearly always damaging and is not in the biblical narrative. Everyone who is a believer is born again by the Spirit (see John 3:5; Titus 3:5) and sealed by the Spirit (see Ephesians 1:13; 4:30). The twelve disciples were specifically instructed by Jesus to remain in Jerusalem until they experienced the filling of the Spirit, even though they had already received the Holy Spirit fifty days prior: "And when he had said this, he breathed on them and said to them, 'Receive the Holy Spirit'" (John 20:22).

So how can we understand being filled with the Spirit? If we already have the Spirit, what does it mean to be filled with Him? How do we know if we have been filled with Him?

I find an illustration particularly helpful here. Every holiday season, I see snow globes decorating people's mantels, desks and coffee tables. No doubt you are familiar with them. They usually have some kind of winter-themed picture or sculpture in the middle, surrounded by a dome of glass that has water and small flakes of white plastic inside. When you shake up the globe, the flakes of plastic stir up throughout the whole space and swirl around, looking like snow falling until they eventually settle on the bottom again.

Before we shake up our globe, the snowflakes are settled at the bottom, mostly out of sight. Shaking the globe forces the snowflakes to fill the *entire* globe. The contrast in this analogy is not one of being full or empty; it is one of being settled or filling the entire space.

The experience of being filled with the Spirit is the equivalent of shaking up the globe. The Spirit who dwells within us is stirred up to influence every part of us. He is no longer affecting only a portion of our humanity. He is permeating our entire being.

This is why the biblical picture is eminently a physical process. There are bodily responses to being filled with the Spirit. We see the filling of the Spirit as an embodied experience because our body is a part of who we are. Much of the time we walk around with the Holy Spirit largely settled in our being. He is constantly communing with our spirit, but we do not always experience Him in the physical or emotional dimensions of our being. When we are filled with the Spirit, however, we experience the Holy Spirit interacting with all dimensions of our humanity.

Biblically, we see that experiencing this often unlocks the gifts of the Spirit to flow more effectively in our lives. This makes sense. If we want the Spirit to move through the laying on of hands, the speaking of our words and the harnessing of our thoughts, we will experience that more freely once we have come into contact with the Spirit in our bodies and minds. He starts the connection in us so He can move through us.

This also helps us understand baptism as Jesus described the experience. When the disciples are filled with the Spirit, Jesus says they have been baptized in the Spirit (see Acts 1:5). It refers not just to immersion but also to influence. For example, dunking a piece of cloth into water would not be baptizing it, but dunking it into dye would be baptizing it, because dye irreversibly alters the cloth. Baptism, therefore, refers not just to any immersion but to *transformative* immersion. In Jesus' definition, baptism is the process of experiencing the Spirit permeating our human-ity, resulting in transformation by Him. It means we are pickled in the Spirit, changed by His saturation of our humanity. We are plugged into a deeper connection with Him and changed more deeply through His increased leverage in our lives.

How do we know if we have experienced a filling of the Spirit? Frankly, I think that is not even a question to get hung up on. Whether or not we have previously had an experience of being filled with the Spirit, Paul's instruction to us is clear: Be continu-ally filled with the Spirit. Let ourselves be overcome with the Spirit (instead of alcohol, in this specific reference) in an ongoing way. "And do not get drunk with wine, for that is debauchery, but be filled [keep on being filled] with the Spirit" (Ephesians 5:18).[1]

Incidentally, we can experience the filling of the Holy Spirit multiple times in our lives, allowing Him to reach our beings at varying levels. It is not a one-time experience. Rather, it is one way the Father imparts His grace for the furtherance of the Kingdom.

So do not get caught up in whether or not you can point to a time you have been filled with the Spirit. Get filled soon. Like the snow in a snow globe eventually settles, our connection with the Spirit tends to wane, and that is a perfect time for a fresh refilling.

Biblically, we see believers being filled with the Spirit both through the laying on of hands (see Acts 9:17; 19:6) and also sovereignly as God initiates (see Acts 2:4; 4:31). I have experienced both personally. I suggest that if you are just getting started with this, have someone pray with you to be filled with the Spirit. There is something powerful about choosing to obey Jesus' command to be filled with the Spirit. It is a wonderful example of the way God loves to link our stories together in the Church.

For a deeper discussion on how to be filled with the Spirit or how to pray for others to be filled with the Spirit, I recommend our School of Kingdom Ministry or the book *Hello Holy Spirit* by Dianne Leman. However long it has been since you have been filled with the Spirit, I encourage you to get a fresh filling. It is how God intends to energize your transformation and mission.

The Dancing Hand of God

The Holy Spirit's presence is sometimes referred to as "the dancing hand of God." That is a wonderful picture of how God touches people as the Spirit blows here and there through our lives. Our job is to recognize the dancing hand of God as the Spirit manifests through His different gifts. As we discussed in the last chapter, we look for the Spirit's hovering presence and then step in and partner with Him.

In my experience, most people actually experience a lot more God activity in their lives than they realize. The dancing hand of God is active all around us, but we have not been trained to recognize it as such. While this is a skill that is "better caught than taught," I would like to offer a few thoughts on how you might get started. This is where the rubber meets the road for the Kingdom of God being released in our day.

While we do not have time to go into depth on each manifestation of the Spirit, we can categorize a few of the gifts and discuss how each functions.

Category	Unifying Purpose	Specific Manifestations
Revelation	Supernatural input that acts similarly to a set of Holy Spirit–empowered senses	Word of Knowledge Word of Wisdom Discerning of Spirits
Inspiration	Supernatural speech in which our words are imbued with God's power	Prophecy Tongues Interpretation of Tongues
Demonstration	Supernatural acts that demonstrate the power of God over the natural order	Gifts of Healings Working of Miracles Faith

Each of these manifestations—revelation, inspiration and demonstration—involves the process of discerning the Spirit's activity and stepping in to partner with what He is doing. God is active. He is involved with our lives. It is *we* who need to learn to tune in and step in. As we do, we will see God's Kingdom enter and influence our world.

The Eyes and Ears of God

Revelation manifestations involve tuning in to our impressions and learning to recognize what, in our experience of ourselves, does not start with us. Each of us is created with spiritual radar to detect things from the spiritual realm, but we may not recognize the activity. Learning to partner with these manifestations is about learning to recognize what is spiritual input and then do something about it (other than brushing it off).

One of the more poignant examples of this is temptation. I have yet to meet a believer who does not experience temptation of some kind, but many of us do not give careful thought to the experience of temptation and what that implies for our perception of the spiritual realm. The Bible asserts that temptation is connected to our own desires (see James 1:13–14) and is also connected to the works of the enemy (see Matthew 6:13).[2] This means that temptation often involves receiving communication from the spiritual realm, but does it feel that way? I do not know about you, but it rarely does for me. To me, temptation almost always feels like my own thoughts.

This is the key. Most of us default to owning every thought that goes through our heads, assuming that it originated with ourselves. That assumption is not true. Often it is God who is inserting His thoughts into our mind as we make our way through our days. You have thoughts injected into your mind from the spiritual realm much more than you might think. So many of the thoughts that come through the mind are dismissed as strange or coincidental. Yet many are actually coming from the Spirit as He whispers to our inner radar.

How then do we know that a thought is or is not from the Lord? At the risk of stating the obvious, whatever is contrary to the Bible or leads to sin is not from God. Something coming into our radar that falls in that category we can chalk up to the enemy immediately.

In other cases, we do not know this until we see the consequences of acting on our impression. I do not know about you, but I would prefer things the other way around—to know if it was God before I did something. God, however, is perfectly comfortable keeping me in a place where I have to trust, act in faith and step out while not entirely sure if it is Him. He has actually been doing that for a long time. Consider His words to Moses at the burning bush: "But I will be with you, and this shall be the sign for you, that I have sent you: when you have brought the people out of Egypt, you shall serve God on this mountain" (Exodus 3:12).

In other words, "Here is how you know I am sending you to go rescue the Israelites. Trust me; it will work." Pretty steep gamble if you have to go square off with Pharaoh.

As we step into what *may* be God, we learn to recognize God's words to us by the tone of the spiritual voice. We learn to recognize His voice by what it sounds like just as we do with the voices of everyone else: our friends, our boss, our spouse, our children.

One of my first experiences of hearing God highlighted both the risk and reward of stepping into His ministry. After my initial China experience, I threw myself into learning and growing in the ministry of the Spirit. Early on, I *desperately* wanted to hear God on behalf of others. I prayed continually that God would open my perception to hear and share.

One day, at the conclusion of church—this was when I still sat in the back row, not fully accepting what I saw around me—I had a strange sense about one of my friends, who was seated at the end of the same row. I did not know exactly what was happening, but I sensed something out-of-normal, and because of my pursuit of hearing God on behalf of others, I asked God if He was going to speak to me about my friend and if there was something He had for me to share.

He answered: "Tell your friend that I see him right now and that he's like Job. All his friends are trying to give advice and help him, but it's only making it more painful."

What? I thought. *God, I can't say that. That's so un-encouraging. I thought this stuff was supposed to be loving and upbuilding.*

Silence.

I was quickly learning that no reply is an invitation to obedience. So, I swallowed hard and approached my friend, asking him if I could share what I thought God may be telling him. After an embarrassing preface, "I really don't know what I'm doing here," I shared my sense of God's word with him. Then I sought validation.

"I know that's kind of a weird word or whatever. Does that mean anything to you?"

His reply crushed me. "No, not really," he responded flatly.

All the wind for hearing God went out of my sails. I took a huge risk and was totally wrong. Ouch.

About six months later, my friend approached me at the prayer ministry time after church. I could not remember ever seeing my friend respond with a desire for prayer, so I approached him and asked what was going on.

"Do you remember that word you gave me a number of months back when you said I was like Job?" he asked.

"Of course—I doubt I'll forget that," I said regretfully.

"Well, this last year has been the worst year of my life. Everything has fallen apart and it's been so hard. Even God has felt far away, and I've been so confused and broken. If it was not for that word, I would not be at this church and I do not know if I'd be following God anymore."

Tears streamed down his face.

Stunned, I realized the process of learning how to hear God is risky, messy and at times painful, but it is also beautiful and powerful. It is worth the risk of looking foolish to share the life of God's breath. The dancing hand of God truly knows what we need, even when we do not understand exactly what He is saying or how to partner with Him.

What might your experience be when the Spirit speaks to you? Well, it tends to work differently for different people. Some people are more visual; they see mental pictures. Others might hear or read words. Sometimes it can feel like a hunch—something you know deep down inside. God can even speak through casual conversation. Ever have something pop out of your mouth that sounded too good to be you? It probably was.

Any way that God speaks to you personally, I want to encourage you to lean in and practice stepping out with it. Hearing God is usually not hard, though it can often be *scary*. I bless you with the courage to embrace the risks as you learn to recognize God's voice.

The Mouth of God

Inspiration manifestations have to do with the Lord speaking through us. It is the modern-day fulfillment of the promise that one day each of God's people would be prophets (see Numbers 11:29; Joel 2:28; Acts 2:17). The prophet acts as God's mouthpiece—an oracle that God speaks through. Similarly, God longs to put His word in our mouths and speak through us.

To operate effectively in inspiration gifts, we must learn to let speech flow from our spirits to our mouths instead of from our minds to our mouths. Most of our speech flows from the mind to the mouth, but learning to speak by the Spirit is about speaking words from a different source.

There is a unique flow to the gifts of inspiration. It can feel like automatic words, although it does not need to be that way. There is a sense of being carried along as we speak. It is as if we are speaking the current thought, unsure what is coming next until the next thought becomes the current thought. Sometimes we are speaking as we find ourselves thinking; other times we may speak as we hear internally. Either way, we flow as we feel directed, and if we are wise, we will stop when we sense the flow has stopped.

The manifestations of inspiration often feel similar to an artist's creative flow. It is no coincidence that artists talk about feeling inspired. The term *inspiration* comes from being in-spirited. Much of the creative process involves catching things from the spirit realm and giving them expression in words, color, stone, film, music or other media.

Learning to speak God's words in this way can be intimidating because it is so out of control, and that is exactly the point. I have found that yielding to God requires one to be out of control so that God can be in control.

A number of years ago, I prayed for a church friend who had been baptized during the service. She had just come through a rough period in her life where she was far from God. She was now connecting with Jesus in powerful new ways. Her life was being flooded with Jesus' love and power. It was beautiful to see. Because our church usually concludes baptism services by min-istering to the newly baptized brothers and sisters, I stepped into the prayer huddle formed around her.

As I prayed, I felt words coming out of my mouth: "Your story is just the beginning of what God is doing in your family. God is going to save your whole family. You are just the first fruit."

It is the kind of prayer you wish you could pull back into your mouth after it leaves. I mean, it is exciting, but it is not something you can make happen. Of course, God can.

After that prayer session, I forgot about the prophetic word I shared with her (I pray for a lot of people). A few years later, the same friend came up to me with her mom, who had recently come to faith in Jesus. Thrilled, my friend reminded me of the prophecy and shared another example of the promised redemp-tion of her family. She said she was praying into that prophetic word and that God was doing amazing things with it. Encouraged, I blessed her mother and told my friend to keep praying.

Earlier this year, I got this text from her: "Fresh off the press. My cousin and her stepdaughter got saved today." When I asked her how many that was now, she told me she needed to think carefully to count them all. At least fifteen, maybe twenty in her family, she said. There were only a few remaining that she was praying for, and her hometown was being transformed by all that God was doing through her family as they came radically to Jesus.

It is scary to allow ourselves to be God's mouthpiece. It is an out-of-control experience, and it involves saying things you may later regret and have to clean up. Do not make the mistake of thinking every time we attempt to prophesy we are entirely accurate. At the same time, do not miss the fruit of prophecy just because you are not perfect and might need to own some mistakes. When all is said and done, it is a much lower risk than the potential payoff.

God's Outstretched Arm

Demonstration manifestations are the hand of God in action. Where revelation manifestations are Spirit-empowered senses, and inspiration manifestations are Spirit-empowered speech, demonstration manifestations are Spirit-empowered actions. They are things we *do* that cause things to *happen*. As such, the doorway to demonstration manifestations is often our motivations or inclinations.

We see an example of this in the life of Gideon, a man who, until this point, had been timid and fearful to embrace God's call. "But the Spirit of the LORD clothed Gideon, and he sounded the trumpet, and the Abiezrites were called out to follow him" (Judges 6:34).

At this point, the Spirit comes on Gideon and drives him to do things he would not otherwise do. Instead of backing down from a gathering army, he steps out boldly, blows his trumpet and calls people to fight with him. His impulse has changed from retreat to advance. In stepping into that impulse, he creates room for God-empowered activity. We see a similar thing with Peter before he walks on water.

> But when the disciples saw him walking on the sea, they were terrified, and said, "It is a ghost!" and they cried out in fear. But immediately Jesus spoke to them, saying, "Take heart; it is I. Do not be afraid." And Peter answered him, "Lord, if it is you, command me to come to you on the water."
>
> Matthew 14:26–28

Peter immediately moves from fear to wanting to walk on the water with Jesus. A dramatic shift. This is what the Scriptures refer to as "moved by the Spirit." It is an internal inclination toward action that is a result of the Spirit driving us from the inside.

Sometimes, inclination comes with such intensity that we feel compelled to action. It can feel automatic. Other times, it is not as strong and feels more like a desire. We just want to do something, not realizing that the desire is coming from the Spirit and not ourselves. Sometimes that desire is a connection to another person—a compassion or sense of draw we feel toward them. Jesus sometimes healed as He was moved by compassion (see Matthew 9:36; 14:14).

Regardless of our experience, the key is to be in touch with, and respond to, what is happening internally. The Spirit's flow requires that we are connected to our inner world, a world that far too many people have closed off because it is saturated with painful feelings or is not self-controllable. When you make yourself out of touch with your inner world, you shut the door to being moved by the Spirit.

God created our inner world because He wants to meet us and move us there. He wants us to learn how to feel His heart in ours and respond as His Spirit blows us along. I find that as I engage my inner world and learn to find God there, He can move me along and demonstrate His supernatural power.

Years ago, I took a number of people from our church on a short-term mission trip to Mexico to minister the love of Jesus. One day, we visited a group of people who make their living through the city dump. These are the poorest of the poor, who gather recyclable material out of the garbage and turn it in for a few coins for a day's labor.

When we arrived at the dump, I was struck by the smell of rotting food and sunbaked diapers. The piles of garbage stretched as far as I could see. As the wind blew, it formed cyclones of garbage in the air. To top it all off, it was over one hundred degrees with no clouds in the sky. As I took it all in, I remember thinking, *This is as close to hell as I've experienced on earth.*

Our team began to find and minister to various workers in the dump—talking, encouraging, praying, sharing food and Jesus' love. I was blown away by my team. They really got it. The Gospel means our humanity is defined not by our circumstances but by what Jesus has done for us. My team spoke to those people in ways that their circumstances did not define. Rather, Jesus' love determined their value and their humanity.

A few friends and I came across a man more elderly than the others. He walked with difficulty, using a cane to navigate the piles of trash while bending over to pick up a scrap here or there. I knew we had to pray for this man.

We approached him and asked if we could pray. He said he had some hip pain and that is why he used a cane. We prayed and asked him if he felt any different. He did not. Puzzled—Jesus is especially quick to heal the poor—I asked for clarification. In response, the man expounded on his injury, saying that he once had an accident and now was left with pins in his hip that caused the pain.

The next words tumbled out of my mouth: "Oh, you don't need your muscles healed. You just need new bone. Let's pray again."

My confidence stunned me. *Did I just say we would pray that metal pins turn back into bone?*

I put my hands on the man's hip and commanded the pins to turn back into bone and for his hip to be fully restored. A few seconds into the prayer, something dropped onto the group with such intensity that I could barely force out the words.

"Hips . . . be . . . restored . . . turn . . . back . . . into . . . bone."

I stuttered under a weight that I knew my friends were also feeling.

After a minute of prayer, we asked the man to check out his legs. He turned around confidently, handed us the cane and walked fifteen feet with ease before returning to us. He verified the pain was gone and that his strength had returned. Later, on our way out, we noticed he had converted his walking cane into a spear to pick up garbage without having to bend over.

The Spirit of God is no less powerful today than He has ever been. God's power is still active on the earth. He is looking for people who will partner with Him to enact His will.

A Lifelong Journey

In this chapter, we have talked about just a few pointers for the beginning of a lifelong trek. We will never know all there is about partnering with the Holy Spirit, because it is a relational journey and there is always more of God to know. This is good. You will never cross it off your list, and that means your whole life will be spent in pursuit of knowing more of God.

Whether you are just learning about the ministry of the Spirit or you have been learning and growing in this area, I want to invite you afresh to that for which you were created. We have been created to cooperate and partner with the Holy Spirit. "For all who are led by the Spirit of God are sons of God" (Romans 8:14).

When we undertake the journey of partnership with the Holy Spirit, we are aligning with our destiny. I can tell you from experience that there is nothing else as fun, challenging, fulfilling, humbling and rewarding as partnering with the living God to see His Kingdom come.

In the context of our individual lives, we can see how these tools arm us to partner with the Holy Spirit to release the Kingdom. Next, let us return to an earlier thread: How does God's Kingdom intersect our world societally? We know God is working to redeem both lives and nations, so how can we step into partnership in the more collective sense? To understand this, we need to take a step back and study the task of the modern Church.

IMPACT POINTS

- Partnership with the Holy Spirit effectively starts with being filled (and refilled) with the Spirit.
- The manifestations of the Spirit fall generally into three categories: manifestations of revelation (Spirit-empowered senses), inspiration (Spirit-directed speech) and demonstration (Spirit-unleashed power).
- Each manifestation of the Spirit involves a different way of tuning in to what is happening in our present moment and connecting with what God is doing.

THE TIMES
THEY ARE A-CHANGIN'

BY EVERY MEASURE I can think of, the Church in the West is failing at our mission.

The general opinion is that faith is becoming less and less central to people's lives. Church attendance is heading downward, churches are closing faster than they are being planted, and many of the popular voices for faith in our day seem to be trending toward a faith that is not compatible with what Jesus taught.

While each of these trends is disconcerting, none of them encapsulates our mission. The mission, as Jesus has mandated it to us, is not captured within church attendance or even faithfulness to orthodox theology. We need those things, but they are not the mission. The purpose of the Church in our day extends beyond these concerns. We are meant to fulfill what Jesus calls us to do. "Go therefore and *make disciples of all nations*, baptizing them in the name of the Father and of the Son and of the Holy Spirit, teaching them to observe all that I have commanded you. And behold, I am with you always, to the end of the age" (Matthew 28:19–20, emphasis added).

This calling is so audacious that many of us have missed it entirely. Notice Jesus' language. He did not say to make disciples *from* all nations but rather to make disciples *of* all nations. By focusing on the individual story, we have missed the broader story. The mission of the Church is to be the redemptive nation that delivers the nations of the world from the broken ways of society perpetrated by fallen gods.

God's desire has always been for the nations. Jesus has always been the hope of the nations, and the Church has always been called to the nations. That means the Church in each country has a clear mission: disciple the nation we call home. Sadly, according to this mission, the Church in the West is falling dismally short of the target.

Now, do not get me wrong. To disciple a nation does not mean to *run* the nation. I am not advocating a Constantine approach where we seek to fill all the roles of societal influence with believers (although a few more would not hurt). Rather, I am suggesting that it is our task to facilitate the leavening role of the Kingdom as described by Jesus. "He told them another parable. 'The kingdom of heaven is like leaven that a woman took and hid in three measures of flour, till it was all leavened'" (Matthew 13:33).

The Church is not the Kingdom, but we are the community that proceeds from the Kingdom. It is our job to stand for and facilitate Kingdom purposes. God has a design and a purpose for every nation, and His ways are the best ways to run any nation. The Church is the storehouse of God's wisdom and revelation, but right now what we have is seen as irrelevant to address the cultural issues of the day. The Church is perceived as backward and resistant, judgmental and opposed to progress. Rarely are the realms of academics, politics, media or healthcare coming to the Church asking for our opinion. There are groups controlling the discussions of our day, and often the Church is not even invited to the table.

I believe this decreasing influence and sense of futility points toward a critical revelation for the Church. In this chapter, we are going to take a slight detour and ask this question: How is God establishing His rule *right now*? What is being established in the world today?

Looking through the Lens of History

While the situation may seem dire, if we have the eyes to see it, the Lord is actually positioning us to do incredible things. The Church has been here many times before, and the lens of history informs us that it is often the darkest moments that precede the new dawn. Death is always followed by resurrection in the Kingdom of God.

As of the time of this writing, we have recently passed a momentous anniversary in the realm of Church history. On October 31, 1517, a young monk named Martin Luther nailed 95 theses to a church door in Wittenberg, Germany. He was not intending to be the spark that caught the world aflame with new ideas, but rather to enter into honest dialogue about the truths he asserted were found in Scripture. Nevertheless, his thoughts were a tipping point for a change in values for much of Western culture.

Martin Luther believed something unheard of in his day: that in Jesus Christ, God made Himself accessible to each and every one of us. The idea does not seem shocking now, but that is because it is actually quite hard for us to even imagine the world in which Luther lived. Those in the church hierarchy—including priests, cardinals and the Pope—were the only people who connected with God. Everyday people did not. Their role was to attend mass faithfully—it was conducted in Latin, a language they did not understand—and believe what the priest told them. After all, he was connected to God for them. Their mission was to live their lives following his instructions for how to keep their eternal destiny secure.

Luther upended this system wholesale. He believed God desired to know each person intimately, and that through Jesus, all people had direct access to God. They did not need a priest to talk to God for them; they could talk to God themselves. They could read His Bible and know Him personally. In short, Luther did not just adjust the accepted understanding of faith in his day. He was the catalyst for an entirely new paradigm.

Luther's paradigm initially revolutionized the expression of the local church, resulting in church services that were conducted in the spoken language of the time (both sermons and hymnody). Church now became applicable and relevant. The Scriptures were translated into the common languages of the day, which resulted in a massive growth in literacy. For the first time in history, there was a book—the Bible—that the everyday person wanted to read. If you were a farmer living in the medieval age, learning to read was a major endeavor. Time spent reading was time not working the fields or tending livestock. For most people, there simply was not much of a reason to learn to read. That attitude changed massively when people learned that God Himself had written a book intended for them to read, the purpose being to come to know Him personally.

The shift continued to ripple through culture into economics and politics. The idea that God wants to know each of us personally implies that each of us has an intrinsic value. If God values each human being, a society ought to reflect that. Individuals, therefore, should have the opportunity to make their lives the best they can be. Each person has personal rights that are intrinsic to who he or she is, because God values each of us. The thought that each person's voice counts in the governing of a culture led to the ideas that are influencing much of the globe today—capitalism and democracy.

The period of time when all this change resonated through the Church is called *the Reformation*. It was a tense and violent time. Wars were fought, people were burned at the stake over their beliefs, and the course of the world was radically altered.

A Lesson from Science

As a physicist, when I study the Reformation, I see a time when the Church went through what I would call a *phase transition*. If you will remember back to your science classes in school, a phase transition is when a solid turns to liquid, or liquid to gas. The iconic example is when ice melts into water.

A phase transition is a fascinating event because it results in a massive change in behavior, even though the underlying ingredients are exactly the same. H_2O (water) molecules are exactly the same above and below the freezing point; nothing in the molecules or the way they behave individually changes at all. What changes is how they are organized. In ice, these molecules organize themselves into neat hexagonal patterns, whereas in water, they are piled on top of each other and move freely like balls in the ball pits at McDonald's where I played when I was young. That change in organization results in a massive difference in the large-scale behavior of the substance, hence the difference between a solid and a liquid.

This is the type of change I see in the Church—and through it, the world—because of the Reformation. There was nothing that changed about the essence of the Christian faith itself. Faith was exactly the same before and after the Reformation. Rather, it was the structure that changed. The way the Church was organized shifted dramatically. That transformation eventually drove big changes in the rest of society.

Two things we learn through the physics of phase transitions are very interesting.

First, phase transitions are precipitated by outside conditions. The water molecules do not decide to melt. Instead, the surrounding temperature creates an environment that drives the phase transition to water.

Second, phase transitions happen as the current order of molecular organization breaks down. Only through the disintegration of the current levels of structure is it possible for the new organization to emerge. In the case of ice to water, the molecules change from a rigid, crystalline structure to be like those free-flowing balls where people lose their kids for hours.

These are the exact conditions at play in the Reformation. While Luther contributed his ideas at a critical time, the cultural context was driving toward a needed change. Luther had the right ideas, but those ideas also needed to intersect with the right times for them to be received. In Luther's day, many factors combined to foster the Reformation. The Church's grip was lessening on culture. People were finding the corruption and deception of the Catholic Church less and less tolerable. The overall dissatisfaction with the religious status quo, the discovery of the new world of the Americas, the beginning of the Renaissance, all combined with a disruptive technology that allowed ideas to spread like never before—the printing press.

These were the driving factors that made a phase transition in society inevitable. When change finally occurred, the violence and civil unrest were the results of breaking down the current organization to make room for the next.

One last observation: Not all churches, or society at large, took the journey with Luther. There still exists the Catholic Church and various Orthodox churches, and there still are portions of society that have not adopted the values and organizational principles that were birthed by the Reformation. Like icebergs floating in water, our world is complex enough to support multiple phases of organization simultaneously.

Types of Relationships

As a parent, I have educated myself in how people develop relationally. My goal is to fully equip my children to live a successful life and make a meaningful contribution to society. As I have studied relationships to learn how we grow, there seems to be a fairly universal pattern. We grow from dependent to independent and finally to interdependent relationships.

When it comes to parenting, we see the pattern clearly. When our children are first born, they are entirely dependent upon us. They need us for food, drink, clothing and so on. As they grow, however, they begin a process of moving from dependence to independence. Parents empower their children to meet their own needs. We teach them to hold a fork and feed themselves, and in time we let them cook. We initially change their diapers, but then we potty train them. We start out dressing them but soon discover they have a fashion sense of their own.

The transition to independence culminates in the teenage years, a time when independence is the main focus. Self-reliance is a huge need, and the fervent desire to live one's own life free from parents is something to which every teenage alumnus can attest. In the independence phase of life, the input of others can feel threatening. We do not know how to maintain our own ideas and identity in the context of others who may think differently. With time, however, we learn to step fully into our own beliefs and values without needing to depend on or resist others' input.

Independence, though, is not the final focus. Only when independence has been firmly established can we proceed to the next level: interdependence. In the interdependence phase, we do not need others. Instead, we learn a relational paradigm that works differently. We welcome relationship with others because it improves our lives and their lives. Free of needing others, we are now able to pursue relationship with others without compromising our values or our identity. A healthy interdependence is the target for parenting. At this point, our children are ready to live as healthy adults in our culture.

As a pastor, I see people go through these same phases spiritually. When people first get saved, their spiritual lives are largely dependent on their home churches. They learn and grow and experience life through the context of the Christians around them. In time, they develop their own spirituality, and their relationships with their churches shift. I can always tell when people are entering this phase because they say things like, "I'm just not getting fed here like I used to." This sentiment reveals that God is moving their spirituality into the next chapter. Unfortunately, many people do not recognize this as a healthy step forward in their spirituality because dependence is always more comfortable than independence.

Spiritual teenagers act a lot like natural ones. As a believer develops her own connection with the Lord and no longer *needs* the Church to stay in touch with God, her focus can become self-centered. She can grow to expect the Church to support unilaterally her passion or sense of calling instead of looking for a healthy partnership. She may even try to tell the leadership what to do in an attempt to access the benefits of the Church without the posture of mutual service and partnership.

In time, though, God brings us through to a place of interdependence where we gladly make our home at a local church, not because we need it to maintain fellowship with Jesus, but because it enriches our lives. We love being connected to God's bride, and we love bringing our part to the Body of Christ as well as experiencing the contribution of others.

An Interdependent Church

The Reformation largely drove the Church from dependence to independence. Before the Reformation, faith was expressed in a mostly dependent way. Churches taught what the Pope told them to teach. People were dependent on the priest for a connection with God. Faith could not be expressed or experienced without the guidance of clergy. Without the intervention of the official Church, there was no connection with God.

The Reformation changed that dynamic and drove the expression of faith in the emergent Protestant Church into independence. The name itself captures the spirit—"protest-ant," meaning *I am going to hold onto my beliefs and nothing you can say or do will change them.* Sounds like a teenager, right? This independent focus created the ideas of a "personal relationship with God" and knowing Jesus as our "personal Lord and Savior." Notice the entire focus for faith is individual. Organizationally, this independent mindset has resulted in the creation of tens of thousands of denominations, including the famous "non-denominational church," a church fully independent of any outside influence.

As believers in Christ, our stance toward our communities is marked by a Protestant sense of independence. For example, we view our cities as projects where we seek to remedy the corrupted populace sinking into the mire of depravity. We think it is our job to "fix" our communities rather than learn to love our communities. Instead of participating in discussions with them, we either resist outside viewpoints or attempt to conquer our communities for ourselves, thinking: *When their culture completely goes to pot, then finally they'll wake up and realize they need what we have. Then they'll see that we have what truly mattered all along.* Unfortunately, our posture is antagonistic and self-aggrandizing. It is the same posture we see with teenagers toward their parents. *What do they know? I'll show them!*

While our culture was transitioning from dependence to independence through the Reformation, the Church led the way and the nations were discipled. In our times, a subsequent shift is happening. Our culture is being driven from independence to interdependence, and unless the Church is willing to step into another Reformation, we will be an echo from the past rather than a guiding voice into the future.

We stand at a critical crossroads in human history. For the first fifteen centuries of the Church, the world was slowly growing and developing as the leaven of the Kingdom leavened the world. When the time came to step into independence, the world was led by a Church that bravely went through a phase transition and modeled for society another echelon of principles and values. We have now experienced twenty centuries of the Kingdom leavening our world, and it is barreling toward an interdependence never before comprehended.[1]

The deck is stacked for another phase transition. The established ways of doing church are breaking down. Today's faith paradigm is not compatible with where God is leading the world. It is irrelevant and out of touch.

We are also experiencing a disruptive technology. This time, rather than being one that champions ideas and individual behavior, as the printing press did, this technology is connective in nature. Our ability to instantly connect anywhere in the world is something people could not have dreamed of a century ago.

The Lord has prepared this time for us, a time to fully live out our role as a body in a way that has never before been possible. For the first time in human history, the Church actually has the capability to be fully connected across the entire globe. "For just as the body is one and has many members, and all the members of the body, though many, are one body, so it is with Christ" (1 Corinthians 12:12).

We are members of one another (see Ephesians 4:25), but our independent relational paradigm prevents us from experiencing it. The Lord sees us as a body, but we see ourselves as a bunch of distinct churches. As a result, our ability to reach our mission suffers (I will share more on this in chapter 11).

What Lies Ahead

If this is true, we have interesting and pivotal days ahead. I cannot claim to predict the details of how everything will shake out, but from the study of history and science, there are a few things we can expect as general features.

Societal Structures Will Continue to Shift

Phase transitions are driven by shifting organizational dynamics. As society continues on the path toward interdependence, the driving organizational structures will continue to change. We have seen early traces of this already. With the internet and the interconnectivity it empowers, some of the traditional rules of how nations relate to one another are shifting. A trade agreement between two countries, for example, is no longer something that can easily be controlled, given the level of cybersecurity and cyber currency that is currently available. Money now follows the internet as much as it does national legislation.

Furthermore, corporations are growing to where they rival nations in scope and influence. Consider Apple Inc. At the time of this writing, Apple is valued at almost one trillion dollars. That is more than the GDP of 170 separate countries. Unlike a nation, though, Apple is global, so it does not belong to any single economy or legislation. Further, let us not fool ourselves with nationalist thinking. A significant number of people feel more commitment and passion toward Apple than their nation. Apple is driving the course of the world at a scale equivalent to a nation but in a totally different way.

The Gospel Will Emerge in a Form Different from What We Have Ever Seen Before

In this entire discussion, we must remember that God is driving the course of history. The world is approaching interdependence because God is preparing the Church to leaven the world in a way never before possible. The only message with the power to drive culture and society toward God's design is the Gospel. During the Reformation, the framing of the Gospel drove the values that dictated the new structures of culture, and the same will occur in the next chapter of human history.

Of course, it is not that the Gospel has changed. The Gospel has not changed at all. Rather, our understanding is developing. The fact is, there is no room within the typical understanding of the Gospel to even move toward interdependence. The entire framing of Jesus' message is around individual salvation. We are individually guilty before God, and so we individually come to know Him. Individuals spend eternity either with the Lord or without Him. Everything is couched in terms of individuality. There is nothing in this approach that can inform an interdependent set of values.

In parallel with how an individual stacks interdependence upon a foundation of independence, if the Church is going to transition to an interdependent paradigm of the Gospel, it too will be built upon the foundation of the past.

It is not that we will abandon the Gospel as we know it. Rather, God will build a greater understanding, one more comprehensive and robust, to complete the Gospel as we now understand it. To step into the future, we will need to allow the Lord to reframe the Gospel for us and take us to a new place. Only armed with that will we be able to meaningfully disciple the nations in the way they need right now.

Church as We Know It Will Begin to Look Very Different

What will the interdependent Church look like? I do not know. I do know that it will look different from what we are used to. When you are part of an ice cube, the idea of liquid water seems unfathomable. The H_2O you know is rigid, not fluid. No other state could be possible. Similarly, whatever state the Church transitions into will likely be something very different from what we have seen in the past. That is okay; it is even good. Remember, the model—the particular ecclesiology—is not the Church. How we practice our faith is not identical to faith itself.

The journey will be rough, and sometimes our steps will be forward and other times backward. That is the nature of innovation; it is messy. What will prevail, however, is a structure of the Church that facilitates an interdependent paradigm of faith. At the least, 1 expect it will involve our faith being integrated into the journeys of other people in some deeper way.

Not Everyone Will Want to Move Forward

Human beings generally do not love change. Tension, uncertainty and conflict are not things to get excited about. Not every community of faith will embrace the new paradigm. This phase transition will split the Church before it is done. Indeed, it has to. The new phase will be incompatible with the old. "And no one puts new wine into old wineskins. If he does, the wine will burst the skins—and the wine is destroyed, and so are the skins. But new wine is for fresh wineskins" (Mark 2:22).

While 1 hate the thought of schisms, they are the unfortunate reality of change. These are times for courage and adventure, not safety and security. Those who push into the new cannot make inclusion of those clinging to the old a necessary outcome of the journey. Water is not ice, and ice is not water. To cling to ice is to choose not to become water.

The World Needs the Leavening Influence of the Kingdom

As culture surges into something new, it needs the Church to provide guiding principles. God is the designer of every phase. He has made both independence and interdependence. Culture will stumble its way through the process one error at a time and eventually find its way toward measures of God's truth, but it is the Church to whom truth rightfully belongs. Without truth, the world merely has a method of trial and error, and every misstep could ruin multitudes of lives. God has given the Church a critical role here. If we do not fully embrace our appointed place, there will be a heavy cost.

Historic Times

These are historic times in which everything is changing. At the moment of a phase transition, more change happens than everything leading up to that point. Ice changes as its temperature gradually moves from below zero to the melting point, but that change is nothing compared to how it changes at the instant it melts into water. All the change that has led up to that point is insignificant compared with the change in the phase transition itself.

When we look at such uncertainty, it is easy to become anxious. The world seems to be spinning out of control, and I am telling you that it is going to get worse before it gets better. Yet, let us not forget an important detail: God is the one driving this process forward. God is the one bringing us into this phase transition. God is the one birthing the conditions necessary in the world to bring the Church forward in a new measure of radiance, brilliance and Christlikeness.

God has chosen us to live in this historic hour. We have been selected to participate in a pivotal season of change unlike any other in the course of history. We have an opportunity to partner with God and influence the world in a way that transcends past changes. I know I am painting a serious picture here. I am saying the entire world is in a state of flux and that God has designed the Church to step in at this hour. It is hard to think on a grander scale and a greater impact than this.

I believe the Lord has given us a prophetic sign of His intention in this hour, although I see it in a most unlikely place. A few months ago I was talking with the Lord about my generation. I am an early Millennial, and while I do not identify with every trait that is typically Millennial, I certainly have a passion to see God move in my generation. While praying, I found myself complaining to the Lord about some of my generation's weaknesses: a tendency toward irresponsibility, a lack of discipline, unrealistic expectations and so forth. As I shared, I felt the Lord speak something very unexpected.

"Do not buy culture's negative assessment of your generation, Putty. Every generation has its problems and its imperfections. Do not miss the point. The Millennials are a *sign*."

"What?" I responded, shocked.

"There is a millennium in the Bible, Putty. What is that millennium about?"

"Umm . . . it's about the uncontested rule of Christ."

"That's right. And I have made the world name this generation the Millennials so that every time someone refers to them as such, it is a reminder of their calling to see the rule of Christ released in this world in a way completely different from what has been seen before."

I was floored. I am still floored when I think about that. God has named this generation Millennials as a prophetic sign of the change in our times. Now, do not hear what I am *not* saying. I am not announcing the millennial rule of Christ, and I am not suggesting this has anything to do with the end times. I am just saying that God has made even the world announce His calling over this time.

This is the time the Church needs to rise up. This is the time for courage and tenacity, for boldness and resolve. It is the time to rise up into the dreams God has for the world and to step into truth, to become truth that the world can see and follow as the ways of God.

IMPACT POINTS

- The conditions in the world in our day look similar to the cultural conditions in Europe before the Reformation.
- In the Reformation, the Church discipled the culture as the world transitioned more fully into a set of societal values centered around independence.
- The Lord is preparing the Church of our day to transition into a form oriented around a more interdependent set of values. When that happens, the Church may once again disciple culture toward the ways of the Lord.

THE TRIUNE GOSPEL

I AM AN AVID GAME PLAYER. I love the challenges, riddles and strategies that come with playing, and it is all the better when I can share it with friends. While growing up, I spent more than my share of time in front of the TV adventuring through various Nintendo characters. Now that I have grown up, most of my game playing has shifted to playing board games (except for sharing a few video games with my son, who is quite excited to play with his dad).

I have always taken my game purchases seriously, as there are always more games out there than there is time to play or money to buy them. I do my homework. I research the most popular games, read reviews, sometimes even watch how-to-play videos to get a sense of whether or not this particular game is a good purchase. When I finally pull the trigger on a specific game, it is always thrilling to be able to open the game, touch the colorful parts and learn the rules.

Almost every game is fun the first few times you play it. Learning how the game works and the experience it creates is rewarding. After the first few plays, though, some games retain the excitement and others seem to lose it. There are classics that you can play dozens or hundreds of times, and there are other games that always seem to get passed over for something more interesting.

Whether you play board games or not, we are all familiar with the experience of getting something we have looked forward to, maybe even dreamed about, and when it becomes ours we find the novelty wearing off. Maybe it is a car, a relationship or your kind of toy. Maybe a vacation or hobby. Whatever the case may be, we have all had the experience of something not quite turning out as we had hoped. What seemed would help us transcend the everyday doldrums turns out to be part of normal life after all. The newness wears off, the enthusiasm wanes and we move on to other interests.

Our journey of faith can be the same way. When we surrender our lives to Jesus, we experience being made new. Everything is so dynamic, so exciting. This is what we have been looking for our whole life. Everything seems more vibrant and our life seems so full. We are over-the-top enthusiastic about Jesus and our faith. We dive in as deep as we can because of how good it is.

Eventually, though, we begin to experience setbacks: places where our faith does not seem to provide answers, challenges we do not know how to navigate, chronic frustrations for which our faith does not give a solution. Maybe not in the first few years, but over time our enthusiasm becomes tempered, and while our faith is a good thing in our life, it is not the incredible journey we first thought it was. Consequently, we come to expect less and ask less.

An Incomplete Story

I cannot help but think this is not the way faith is supposed to work. Our faith is the one part of our lives that *should* transcend the normal and always be thrilling. Why? Because in God there is always something new. There is always more to discover and walk in. God is the most incredible being in the universe; there is infinite depth in knowing Him. He never gets old.

So why does our faith seem to go stale with time? I want to propose a radical answer: It is because we do not have the complete story. The Gospel is the centerpiece for our journey of faith, and if we do not have the entirety of the Gospel clear, our faith will not be applicable when we need a missing portion. It is like a partial map, a half-written recipe or a puzzle missing pieces. It is enough to get somewhere, just not enough to reach where we should.

The Gospel is God's good news—the news that God Himself is excited about. It is the most thrilling, wondrous thing we can set our minds on. We should find ourselves daydreaming about it just because we enjoy thinking about it. It ought to be the fuel to encourage ourselves and the source of our enthusiasm when we wake up in the morning. If the Gospel is less than that, surely it is not because God's good news is lacking. No, it is because our version of the Gospel does not match His. We might have the Gospel, and even nothing but the Gospel, but we do not have the whole Gospel. Just as a partial truth can be misleading in a court of law, a partial Gospel will leave us lacking in our Christian life.

I believe the Church has inadvertently truncated the Gospel through unrealistic expectations. In an attempt to reach people for the Kingdom, we simplify the message, trying to make it clear enough for new believers to follow Jesus. Certainly, clarity is good, but the fact is that none of us gets saved with a complete understanding of what we are getting into. We get saved with a partial picture of the Gospel; indeed, it is not even possible to truly comprehend the Gospel without experiencing the new birth and the empowering of the Spirit. In this noble aim to reach others for faith, we present an abbreviated Gospel while inadvertently portraying this snapshot as the complete Gospel.

Not only does this introduce problems for our personal journey of faith, it fails to equip us for our role as the Church in society.
We need a Gospel that arms us as individuals to deal with personal evil while simultaneously releasing the Church to deal with
societal evil. Anything less is to sell short Jesus' Kingdom mission.

In this chapter, I would like to offer some direction in framing
the Gospel based on the last chapter. As we will see, this Gospel
framework is connected to, and supports, the Kingdom message
we have been exploring in this book.

I know it would be prideful to think I alone have uncovered the
core message of the future church. Many people are contributing
to this subject. Still, I want to be involved in the conversation,
and so I offer my thoughts to the dialogue. Certainly, what I offer
is not complete nor perfect; hindsight will judge my accuracy. In
the meantime, please consider my humble contributions to this
great conversation.

A Three-in-One Gospel

The Gospel of Mark is generally accepted as the first gospel written. At the beginning of Jesus' ministry, we read in Mark the message Jesus shared: "Now after John was arrested, Jesus came into
Galilee, proclaiming the gospel of *God*" (Mark 1:14, emphasis
added).

Notice the language: the Gospel of *God*. The core of the good
news is connected to who God is. Not just forgiveness, freedom
or what He has done for us, but fundamentally *who He is*. It is
out of His nature, after all, that He acts. His actions flow from
who He is. This phrasing actually occurs a number of times in the
New Testament (see Romans 1:1; Romans 15:16; 2 Corinthians
11:7; 1 Thessalonians 2:8–9). Furthermore, there are a number
of phrases along the lines of the "gospel of Christ" or "gospel
of Jesus" (see Mark 1:1; 2 Corinthians 2:12; 2 Corinthians 9:13;

2 Corinthians 10:14; Galatians 1:7; Philippians 1:27; 1 Thessalonians 3:2; 2 Thessalonians 1:8).

I find this interesting because we usually associate the Gospel with what God has done more than with who He is. We tend to define the Gospel by words like "grace" or "forgiveness"— descriptions of what has happened or how things work now. There is a strong thread in the New Testament, however, that the Gospel is *God Himself.* Who God is—this is the good news.

Once we begin to examine the nature of God in the Scriptures, we discover a counterintuitive picture—a deep mystery called the Trinity. In short, the Trinity depicts God as existing in community. There are three persons to the Trinity: the Father, the Son and the Holy Spirit. They are equal and eternal. Each of them is fully God and fully distinct from the others, yet we do not have three Gods. We only have one God. It is a mind-bending paradox, but after some thought, not an unexpected one. Should we not expect the nature of God to be difficult for our mortal minds to understand? Indeed, it is the complexity that invites a journey. We get to spend the rest of our lives exploring the depth of this paradox as we come to know God both now and in eternity.

While diving deeply into the intricacies of the Trinity is beyond our present discussion, there is one visual depiction of the Trinity that I find helpful. It is called the shield of the Trinity because it was literally put on the shields of knights in the medieval era.

If the Gospel is about who God is, then the Gospel must be wrapped up in the Trinity as well. God's nature is complex and profound, so we must expect the Gospel of God to be complex and profound. If we have a three-in-one God, we should expect to have a three-in-one Gospel. The Gospel and God have the same shape. In fact, I would suggest the Gospel *has* to have the same shape as God because of how Christianity works. Our salvation is *relational,* not doctrinal. We are saved through the context of relationship with God, not correct beliefs. This is why the beginning

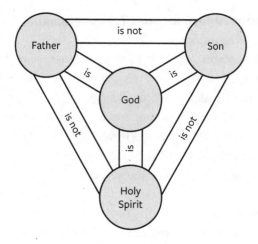

Shield of the Trinity

of our Christian walk is faith, or in other words, trust. Trust opens the door to relationship, and in the context of that relationship, God's grace redeems us.

The Trinity is about one God who is three persons. Three in persons, but one in essence. Now, I do not know about you, but I do not know how to have a relationship with an "essence." I do know how to have a relationship with persons. The result is that functionally we have three different relationships with God: one with the Father, a different relationship with the Son and yet a third with the Spirit. This is why many people feel more connected to, or familiar with, some members of the Godhead than others. It is possible, for example, to have a functioning relationship with Jesus but not really know the Father or the Spirit as well.

In fact, each of these connects and ministers to us in different ways. Paul wrote it this way: "The grace of the Lord Jesus Christ and the love of God and the fellowship of the Holy Spirit be with you all" (2 Corinthians 13:14).

Because we experience each member of the Godhead separately, we should expect that our Gospel consists of one Gospel in three separate stories. Each of these stories is distinct, yet they are each fully the Gospel.

> But I do not account my life of any value nor as precious to myself, if only I may finish my course and the ministry that I received from the Lord Jesus, to testify to the *gospel of the grace of God.*
>
> Acts 20:24, emphasis added

> For I am not ashamed of the gospel, for it is the power of God for salvation to everyone who believes, to the Jew first and also to the Greek. For in it [*the gospel*] *the righteousness of God is revealed* from faith for faith, as it is written, "The righteous shall live by faith."
>
> Romans 1:16–17, emphasis added

> And he went throughout all Galilee, teaching in their synagogues and proclaiming the *gospel of the kingdom* and healing every disease and every affliction among the people.
>
> Matthew 4:23, emphasis added

Each story is the Gospel, but they are not equivalent. They are separate stories, each of them fully the Gospel, but not identical. Yet with all three stories, we have only one Gospel, not three Gospels. Paul is very clear on that point and pronounces a two-fold curse on anyone who steps beyond the single Gospel.

> Not that there is another one, but there are some who trouble you and want to distort the gospel of Christ. But even if we or an angel from heaven *should preach to you a gospel contrary to the one we preached to you,* let him be accursed. As we have said before, so now I say again: If anyone is preaching to you a gospel contrary to the one you received, let him be accursed.
>
> Galatians 1:7–9, emphasis added

153

Succinctly framing what we will continue to unpack in parallel with the shield of the Trinity, here is how we could depict the *Triune Gospel*:[1]

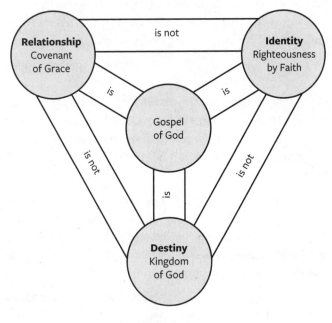

Triune Gospel

Understanding the Stories

The majority of the focus of this book is the Kingdom of God story, but because these stories are interconnected, we need to flesh out each of them. This section gives a brief review. If you would like more depth, consider my previous book *Live Like Jesus*.

Each of these stories traces the full arc of Scripture from Creation through the Fall to the atonement and Gospel proclamation. Each story draws out a different element of the story, and in each story, the life and passion of Jesus fulfill a different function.

The story of grace describes our relationship with God. We are originally made to walk in intimacy and fellowship with the Lord, and it is only out of that fellowship that we can dwell in the identity and destiny God has given us. Whereas we are made for connection, in time the situation falls drastically short of that. At first, there is the turning away from God in the Garden of Eden. Man chooses the knowledge of good and evil over obedience.

In time, the separation is formalized as the Israelites—God's chosen people at the time—find themselves in a covenant called the Law, a covenant of performance designed to keep most of the people out of direct contact to God. There is a priestly class that separates people from accessing the presence of the Lord.

Later, Jesus arrives and institutes a new way of knowing God as Father. He teaches His disciples to pray, "Our Father . . ." When He resurrects, He tells Mary to pass along the message that He is ascending to "my Father and your Father" (John 20:17). Through His death, He acts as the sacrificial lamb required by the Law and pours out His blood to create a new covenant of grace in which we dwell continuously in God's favor and love, never again to be separated.

This is the story many believers think of as the Gospel—a story of sin, judgment, forgiveness and reconciliation.

The story of righteousness reveals our identity—what it means to be human according to God's design. In the very beginning, God speaks over Adam and Eve, saying they are to be made "in our image, after our likeness" (Genesis 1:26). We are made to reveal God—a living, breathing picture that the rest of the world recognizes as God. Yet our humanity is twisted when sin enters the human story. We no longer reveal a pure picture of God because the sin dwelling inside us manifests through us. The crown jewel of creation is corrupted.

Jesus came and revealed the original design. He came as a human being, but one without a fallen nature. He told His disciples,

"Whoever has seen me has seen the Father" (John 14:9). He is the visible image of the invisible God (see Colossians 1:15). He is the picture of the design of humanity. He deals with the sin in us by joining us to Himself and putting to death our old nature through His crucifixion. He follows this by resurrecting us to new life as a new creation through His resurrection. This story is about how Jesus restores us to the original design for our humanity.

The story of the Kingdom defines our destiny. It is the purpose we were created for just as God declared over Adam and Eve's creation. God purposes us to have dominion over all that lives in the earthly realm (see Genesis 1:26). As image bearers of the King, we are given a king's job to do on this planet. When Satan deceives Adam and Eve, he hijacks that authority and begins to exercise his cruel rule on this earth.

Jesus is the challenger to Satan's destructive dominion on this planet. He arrives to destroy the works of the devil (see 1 John 3:8). He is here to upend Satan's authority and take the planet back. Through His own victory over the powers of the enemy, He reclaims the dominion that has been lost both individually and societally, and He sends us out under His authority. We are restored to our original calling under the direction of Jesus Christ. This story is the primary focus of this book.

Each of these stories hinges on the person and work of Jesus. He is the hero in every story. He first comes as the model of the original design. He is in relationship with God as the Son of the Father. He is fully righteous and fulfills the identity that God declared over humanity as God's image bearer. Finally, He comes as the strong man who binds and plunders the enemy's goods. He is destroying the works of the devil.

Not only does Jesus demonstrate the design, He also makes atonement for humankind and restores us to the original design. In the relationship story, Jesus is the sacrificial lamb. He pours out His blood for our forgiveness and makes a new covenant in which we are welcomed home to the Father. In the identity story, Jesus is united with us in death and resurrection. He hangs on the cross as the broken us and kills the sin nature living within us. When He is resurrected, we are born again into new life and made a new creation. In the destiny story, Jesus overthrows the powers of the devil that plague both individuals and society. He reclaims authority in heaven and on earth and pours out His spirit so that we can partner with the Holy Spirit to release God's will on earth again. Jesus is the crux of every story.[2]

As we look forward to our Christian life, each of these stories directs us toward experiencing and interacting with a different member of the Godhead. The story of our relationship is a story of coming home to a loving Father and learning to rest in His embrace. The story of our identity grounds us as a new creation in Christ, compelling us to discover Jesus dwelling within us and ourselves alive in Him. The story of our destiny points us toward the activity of the Holy Spirit and positions us as partners with Him, releasing the Kingdom of God on earth in our day.

One God, three persons. One Gospel, three stories. Just as we will spend the rest of our lives exploring the depth and majesty of who God is, we will also spend the rest of our lives exploring the glorious good news of the Gospel and how it changes everything in our lives.

Without the complete story of the Gospel, we stall out on God's plan to meet our fundamental human needs. The Gospel is meant to complete our humanity, to make us the most deeply human we could be—restored to God's original picture of humanity and living in partnership with Him.

- Does your faith feel dry and logical?
- Does your faith fail to resonate on a deep heart level?
- Do you lack rest, peace and calmness in your life?

- Do you feel alone in your journey?
- Does God seem distant or judgmental?

I believe God is inviting you deeper into the message of His grace toward you. He longs to meet you and saturate your being with His unconditional love and acceptance.

- Do you love Jesus but struggle to value yourself?
- Do you find yourself in competition with others or constantly offended by inconsequential matters?
- Do you hate yourself or your life at times?

I believe Jesus is inviting you into a new picture of yourself as you begin to see yourself through His eyes. He knows who you are better than you do and would love to share His perspective with you.

- Does your faith seem to matter, or has it become something that you continue to do because it is the right thing?
- Are your chief goals merely to be nice and not do wrong things?
- Does life not feel as if you are living an adventure with God?

The Holy Spirit has a life of significance and purpose for you. He has prepared things for you to do and wants your journey of faith to be a thrilling partnership as you partner with God to rebuild the world to match His heart.

Triune Transformation

This chapter barely scratches the surface of the three-in-one Gospel. For a fuller treatment of the scriptural origins of this view and the implications of a paradigm shift in our understanding of the Gospel, again I suggest my previous book *Live Like Jesus*. We do not have space here to fully develop this picture of the Gospel. Yet it is vital to think about the Gospel carefully, deeply and, most of all, biblically, if we are going to do something radical like proposing that the Gospel is not what we have thought it is. In *Live Like Jesus*, I take a number of chapters to walk through the Scriptures and show why we need an updated picture of the Gospel.

For the remainder of our journey here, we will explore how this Triune Gospel supports and informs the Gospel of the Kingdom. The Triune Gospel means not only that we have three stories but also that there is only one Gospel. The three stories are distinct, but they are interwoven and meant to build upon and support each other in God's singularly glorious good news. Like members of the Godhead, these three stories come in one package. Like the members of the Godhead, these three stories support one another and work together.

Our lives—indeed, our very humanity—are designed to be plugged into God. Our heart is not capable of continually thriving without encountering and engaging with the Lord. This union is part of His being the creator and our being the created. As God's good news of great joy to humanity, the Gospel is what gives us what we need to live as we were designed. Like the final puzzle piece, the Gospel is perfectly shaped to fill what is lacking in our life, and this is why it is so important that we have the whole story. Without the entirety of the Gospel, it is impossible to fill what is lacking in our lives. We will try our best, but only God's solution can give us what we need.

God uses the Gospel not only to save us but to transform us into everything He has destined for us. The Gospel is the power of God that brings us into His wholeness (see Romans 1:16). To see how this plays out, let us unpack one more element of the doctrine of the Trinity. While each member of the Godhead is equal and eternal, there is also an underlying structure to the Trinity. The Nicene Creed outlines this as follows:

> We believe in one God,
> the Father, the Almighty, . . .
> We believe in one Lord, Jesus Christ,
> the only Son of God,
> eternally begotten of the Father, . . .
> We believe in the Holy Spirit, the Lord, the giver of life,
> who proceeds from the Father and the Son. . . .

The Father is ungenerated, the Son is begotten of the Father and the Spirit proceeds from the Father and the Son. All three are God and all three are eternal. There was never a time before the Son or the Spirit. These are described in the Nicene Creed as "eternally begotten" and "proceeds."

While this is one of those mind-bending points of the Trinitarian doctrine, thinking about the parallel in the Triune Gospel is actually simple in application. There is an order in which God stacks Gospel truth upon Gospel truth. In the process of our transformation in the Gospel, the story of our identity proceeds from the story of our relationship. The relationship story—the truth that it forms in our lives—provides the foundation for God to build the revelation of our identity in Christ. Similarly, God builds upon what has been formed in our lives through the relationship and identity stories to stack the destiny story on top. These stories fit together and are foundational to one another.

As these stories progressively intersect our lives and culture, they transform our lives and culture, bringing both into alignment with God's design and purposes.

In Romans, Paul highlights this process as the breaking of death's rule over our world. The rule of life is released through us as the Kingdom is stacked on top of the relational covenant

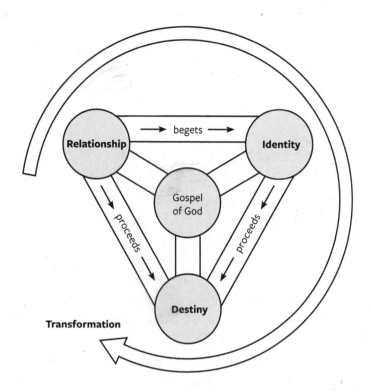

of grace and our new identity as righteous new creations. "For if, because of one man's trespass, death reigned through that one man, much more will those who receive *the abundance of grace* and *the free gift of righteousness* reign [*Kingdom*] in life through the one man Jesus Christ" (Romans 5:17, emphasis added).

Notice Paul's language. If we receive these other things, we can expect to reign in life. Paul is pointing to a process. Indeed, God has a process to build maturity in us, one that reflects His very nature. The Lord is constantly working to layer these stories upon each other, and in so doing, the world is transformed to match His design. This is critical if we want to be people of Kingdom impact. We need to make sure we are well versed not only in the Kingdom story but in the relationship and identity stories as well. To fully step into our task as the Church—to release the Kingdom both individually and societally—we need the tools of the Triune Gospel.

Let us now look at how it applies in our individual lives.

IMPACT POINTS

- The Gospel is God's, and because we know God relationally, we should expect to have three separate relationships with the Godhead and three stories of the Gospel's redemption in our lives.

- Jesus is the key to each story. He reveals the original design of our relationship, identity and destiny, and in His atonement He restores us to what God intended for us in each story.

- These three stories come as a package deal meant to support and reinforce one another both individually and collectively. The Gospel transforms our lives and our world as the relationship, identity and destiny stories stack upon each other in that order.

THE KINGDOM LIFE

FOR AS LONG AS I CAN REMEMBER, I have been enthusiastic about martial arts. Perhaps it was growing up in the age
of Teenage Mutant Ninja Turtles, or maybe it was living in China
when I was young. I am not sure. In any case, for most of my life,
I have loved to punch, kick, spar and swing any kind of weapon.

When I moved to Champaign-Urbana, Illinois, for graduate
school, I joined a Kung Fu school and had a total blast training.
I became one of the more committed and focused senior students in our school, learning not only the basics of hand-to-hand
combat but also how to use staves, the broadsword and straight
sword, the spear, chain whip, three-sectioned staff and more.

Later, our teacher moved away and turned the school over to
me and a few other senior students. Together, we ran the school
for a few years until the rest of them moved away or transitioned
to other hobbies. I continued to run the school alone for a number of years until the challenges of pastoring and parenting forced
me to pass the school on to others. In the years when I ran it,
we became a strong school, competing (and often winning) in
various regional tournaments.

One of the joys I regularly experienced was introducing students to the techniques, focus and discipline required to become a skilled martial artist. Training for battle requires a high level of commitment, one that shapes your whole life. There are skills, activities and a mindset that must become second nature to excel. When taken seriously, martial arts is not just a hobby but something that shapes your personality.

These who want to be effective in any major practice must give themselves to the transformation required to develop high levels of skill. Think of the thousands of hours required to master a musical instrument, or the effort required to learn a new language. These are pursuits that require development as a human being.

God calls us as believers to the Kingdom mission. He calls us to partner with the Holy Spirit and release His rule on the earth. This is a lifelong journey, and like any good trainer, God has a plan to develop not just our ability to partner with the Spirit but our whole lives around the mandate He has given us.

Becoming a World Changer

I love that God provides everything to accomplish that which He asks of us. He never calls us to something for which He does not empower us. It is no different with the Kingdom story. God calls us to become world changers, knowing that we grow into our destiny for our entire lives.

My experience has been that there are two ways people approach living out their destiny as carriers of the message of the Kingdom of God. One set of people leans into the Kingdom with their own enthusiasm and effort. This looks like psyching themselves up to step in and partner with God. We do it because it will be amazing (possibly), or because this is what God is calling us to do. We partner with God, but the motivation is external, not intrinsic; we do things because we think we should or because we have been inspired or motivated to. We are not partnering with God out of the natural overflow of healthy, Spirit-led lives, but by summoning up what we need to create our version of the right thing.

This story often goes like this: A believer encounters an outside influence. Perhaps they go to a conference, read a book, watch a movie or hear an encouraging testimony. This outside input triggers them to make a decision: *I gotta experience this!* The person then steps out with boldness and courage, attempting to partner with the Holy Spirit. Maybe it even works and something amazing happens.

The pattern repeats for a while, but eventually the effect seems to lift. Either the person starts losing motivation or confronts a situation that is frustrating or painful. Someone is not healed or some other embarrassment occurs. In time, the believer reverts back to his or her previous practice and the Kingdom seems out of reach.

I know this scenario well because I have been there. It is hard to walk this story out; it feels frustrating and disappointing. The Kingdom feels like a farce, something that promises a lot but does not deliver on those promises at all. I spent a long time trying to partner with the Kingdom through summoning up enthusiasm. At times things would happen and I would be encouraged, but by and large the journey was mostly frustrating.

Fortunately, there is a second approach to living out the Kingdom calling, one that comes from a different side. It begins with realizing that what Jesus is calling us to is not a product of our own efforts. It is something foreign to this world and the way we live. Jesus intends for us to live from another world and be directed toward this one. That is not something we have the capability to do. He is calling us to the impossible—at least the impossible without His empowering and propelling.

That is okay, however, because with God all things are possible. Once we realize that what God is calling us to is impossible, our task actually becomes easier. When we believe something is simply *hard*, it is common to try to do it ourselves. When we realize that God's calling is not possible unless God makes it possible, we position ourselves differently. We surrender ourselves and look to God for His empowering. We ask God to form us into something different from what we are, because only by being formed into something new can we live out the calling the Lord has given us.

To consistently live out the calling to release the Kingdom means becoming a new kind of person. It means transformation to the point where the Kingdom is our default response. It is not something we summon up, but something that naturally flows from us. God is well able to do that in us if we give Him the room to do so.

The Kingdom is not achieved—it is received. There is a reason the phrase "inherit the Kingdom" is used throughout the New Testament. An inheritance is something we do nothing to earn. It is something given to us. To be a world changer, we need to receive a new way of living so we can consistently receive and release the Kingdom. As we saw in the last chapter, God brings us around through the three stories of the Triune Gospel to release transformation in our lives. In this chapter, we look at how this works personally so we can begin to explore it collectively.

A Model from Maslow

Interestingly, psychology confirms this same process of human development. I guess we should expect such if the findings are accurate. In the mid-1900s, a psychologist named Abraham Maslow studied what humans needed to live as successfully as possible.

In time, he developed what he called a "hierarchy of needs." His theory can be depicted as a stacking set of needs that must successively be met for people to mature to the fullest expression of their humanity:

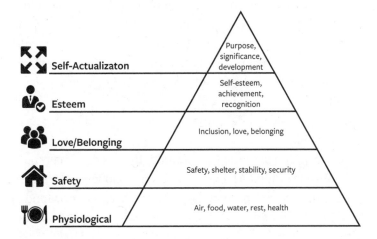

While Maslow was not writing from a religious perspective, I think it is fascinating how his work correlates to the design of the Gospel. Psychology finds that to be fully human, we need exactly what the Gospel provides for us.

According to Maslow, the first need is to have our basic physical, survival needs met: food, water, shelter. Similarly, God calls the Church to be a vehicle for helping people meet this need:

> If a brother or sister is poorly clothed and lacking in daily food, and one of you says to them, "Go in peace, be warmed and filled," without giving them the things needed for the body, what good is that? So also faith by itself, if it does not have works, is dead.
>
> James 2:15–17

It is God's expectation that our faith is demonstrated by our actions to meet the needs of others.

Once our basic survival needs are met, the next need is security—to be safe and out of immediate danger. This implies an environment where we can build our lives without fear of attack or the need to defend ourselves. Yet, what if the need for security extends beyond our immediate lifetime? We have a need not only for physical survival but also eternal survival. This is the next layer of what the Gospel offers: eternal security—knowing all will be well forever. This is the message of salvation, and for most of us, it is the introductory layer of our experience of faith. If we never continue onward to receive more from the Gospel, however, we will not develop into everything God has for us as human beings.

As we continue along the pyramid, the needs remain both natural and spiritual. The next need is for belonging. We have a need to fit in, to be a part of a family, to be loved as we are and to be supported emotionally. Meeting this need is meant to come from our community but also from the Lord. God has made a covenant of grace—a commitment to His favor for us. We will always belong to Him, and we are always in His family. We are at home in His love and always included in His favor. He sees and values who we are, and we are always met with His compassion and loving embrace.

Building upon a covenant of grace, the next need is self-respect. We need to develop a positive self-concept and love ourselves in a healthy way. In this, we come to a place where we believe in ourselves and can begin to define what we want our lives to be. We can stand for our own beliefs and values in the midst of what others may prefer. The biblical root for this is the message of our identity in Christ, which is our righteousness. As believers, our image of ourselves does not need to be provided by ourselves. It comes through understanding what God thinks about us. We are who He says we are. We see ourselves through His eyes.

The final level of the pyramid is significance and purpose. Maslow spoke of self-actualization and self-transcendence as being the fullest representation of ourselves as we live our lives driven by a purpose—something that goes beyond us. As we do that, our life becomes more meaningful and we begin to live for something greater. This is where the message of the Kingdom comes into play. As we partner with the Kingdom story, we enter God's cosmic drama. The purpose of our lives transcends the mortal to the eternal. We live knowing that the purpose we dedicate our lives to now will echo throughout eternity. Indeed, we have taken our place in the greatest story of all.

All of this means that the road to living the fullness of our destiny starts with things that may not immediately appear connected to releasing the Kingdom. It starts with meeting God and allowing Him to form our lives according to His Kingdom purposes. In each area, the goal is to be formed in the Gospel. It is about God orienting these portions of our lives and supernaturally energizing them as we come into contact with Him. We are not talking only about healthy, natural relationships and identity. We are talking about God-connected and God-empowered relationships and identity.

Connecting with the Father

The foundation for all the Gospel's formational work in our lives is connecting with the Father in relationship. We often describe the first step of our journey as "coming into relationship with God." Yet it is not just the first step but a lifelong pursuit that the Lord is constantly growing and establishing. The Father is constantly calling us home to His heart, opening us to living from the embrace of His love defining our experience. If we want to be people of the Kingdom, we must understand this as the foundational layer.

This layer is foundational to the ministry of the Kingdom, because without a strong base of relational connection, our destiny can devolve into a tool for earning God's love. In short, our mission can become a *performance*. Internally, we think: *If I serve God better, I'll experience more of His love.* Such thinking completely undermines the Kingdom mandate. It is self-centered, and love is never self-centered (see 1 Corinthians 13:5). Loving others so we are loved in return is not actually love at all. It is using other people to get what we need. It is manipulation.

God desires to bring us past a performance mentality and into a place where we are secure in His love and able to freely love others because our need for love has been satisfied. We are free from comparison, competition and self-protection. As God develops us into the relationship story of the Gospel, new qualities define our experience of life. Let us examine a few of them.

Meaningful Connection

As the relationship story works out in our lives, we deeply connect with God. He becomes not just an idea out there, or someone we know we should serve and obey, but a person—rather, three persons—with whom we have a relationship. This godly bond becomes meaningful in our lives. Although we cannot see God directly, our connection with God becomes every bit as real as with other people. It becomes the source of our life. It frames our lives and energizes us. When we neglect our time with God, we find ourselves missing Him. He becomes our safest and closest confidant—the One we instantly turn to when things get tough.

Loving Worship

As we build meaningful connection with God, we experience His love for us. His love is not just an abstract idea we read about.

It becomes a part of our reality. We come into contact with the stunning truth that *God is love*, and to know God is to know love. Our heart swells with His love for us, and in return, our love for God multiplies. Worship becomes a natural response, as we are truly only returning the love that God heaps upon us. Worship becomes a lifestyle that we find ourselves doing without intending to do. The more we worship, the more we experience the Lord and bask in His love. We begin to recognize *why* worship is the constant activity of heaven.

The Posture of Our Heart

The relationship story anchors our hearts to the only motive that is valid in the Kingdom: love. We release all our relational agendas and simply love people because we see love as the point. Love becomes the anchor for our hearts, and we learn to quickly sense whether we are walking in love or not. Anything other than love feels foreign, and when we find ourselves outside of love, we are surprised how disrupting it is to our inner experiences. (We likely never noticed that before.) We now walk in love because we do not want to experience anything other than love. The posture of our hearts becomes one of the most important things to us. We grow to be far more concerned about what we are doing internally than what is happening to us externally.

Living in a Family

As relationship with God evolves into the bedrock of our lives, we value relationships in a higher way. Relationship becomes the core of everything we do, and we especially value the family of faith. We see our church not as a group of people who attend the same weekend function but as the group of people God is forming into a family. We love and give to the family, prioritizing it above our individuality. We look for new ways to give to others. We champion others and seek to give them the best portions of our lives. We go out of our way to honor, serve, give to and support others. This becomes natural to us as we genuinely desire to return the life and love we experience from God through His family.

Kingdom Relationships

We become more and more intentional about relationship. Relationships are not merely formed in reaction to circumstances. Instead, we see relationships as an *investment* we are looking to make. We steward relationships with purpose, and we increasingly do relationship according to the way God does relationship with us. We stop holding others to expectations of performing or giving to us in certain ways. We stand up for what we need, but we look to help others get what they need too. Relationships become more the focus than any specific issues, and we relate to others through the value of the relationships even in conflict.

Loving Ourselves

We also grow in our ability to love ourselves because God's love has convinced us that we are lovable. We let go of needing to be perfect or to perform well for ourselves, God or others. We learn to accept ourselves on our worst days and not think less of ourselves when our worst comes out. We see ourselves through the value that God has extended to us. We are valuable because He says so. We are able to just be ourselves, not needing to prove anything or keep busy to distract ourselves from our own presence. We genuinely like ourselves because we are so filled with God's love for us. We stop trying so hard at everything and learn to be more present and have more fun. We laugh, cry and let ourselves feel. We let ourselves be human.

Growing into Christ

Layered upon the foundation of relationship, God works the process of growing us into maturity. Jesus has made each of us a new creation, and now the journey is to learn to live that out to the fullest. Our minds are renewed and we increasingly become living, breathing pictures of Christ dwelling within us.

This layer is critical for us to walk out our destiny, because without an established identity rooted in God's view of who we are, we could wander into anchoring our identity in our calling. We could see our mission as what gives us value or significance, and that without it, we do not seem important. If this happens, it becomes damaging to our journey because, in effect, we are worshiping our calling. It becomes the idol that provides us with self-worth, and as a result, we lack the grace we need to live out what we are called to.

God grows us up in a healthy self-perception in which we see ourselves through His eyes. We see ourselves as defined by His truth, and that extends increasingly into our behavior. Seeing ourselves as He sees us, we are empowered to live out who He says we are. Our lives conform more and more to God's design for humanity as revealed by Jesus.

Scripture

The Bible becomes increasingly significant as a connection point with God. We come to know God not only through relationship but as the God who has been revealed by the Word—the living Word Jesus Christ and also the written Word in the Scriptures. The Bible shifts from confusing to life-giving as we connect its words to our life. The Bible evolves into a source of authority in our lives. What is written carries extra weight as we connect with the fact that God is behind the words. We recognize that God has a *design*, that there is a roadmap called the "ways of God" that has been revealed. These ways of God show how to make good choices and reveal His intention for the entirety of the created order. They show us how to live out the new creation into which we have been welcomed.

Identity

One of the deepest applications of Scripture is seeing ourselves through God's eyes. Our self-definition becomes liberated from the grip of our history, parents, peers and the opinions of others. We perceive ourselves through the lens of who God says we are. Not only are God's ways revealed, but who *we are* is revealed. Our need for self-value finds its resolution in God, not in the messages of our circumstances. Our inner experience is increasingly freed from the situations around us. Our lives take on a new sense of stability and freedom.

Obedience

As the ways of God become more and more clear to us through Scripture, alignment of our lives with God's ways becomes supremely important. Obedience is no longer about "following the rules" but rather about living as close to God's heart as possible. We obey because we love to live the ways of God. We not only flee sin, but we pursue righteousness (the original design) because it is a joy in our hearts to live in alignment with God's design, the design in which we have already been granted participation. We lose any callousness about areas of sin in which we have been apathetic. We take joy in a spotless life because we experience the quality of life that exists when we are not constantly bogged down by sinful choices.

Integrity

As obedience becomes more real to us, we recognize integrity emerging within us. Not just integrity in making good choices when there are other options on the table, but integrity in being faithful to ourselves as the new creations that God has made us. We experience what it means to be whole. Our righteous natures align with desires for the good, and this is reflected by righteous behavior. That lack of division within our humanity releases a spiritual authority through us; we begin to walk in the power of *being*—specifically of living as someone made by God. We become whole people, inside and out. We shine as light in the spiritual darkness of the world. We walk according to God's design in a world that has lost the design. We have wisdom the world lacks.

Discernment

The knowledge of God and His ways produces in us a discernment that guides our journey. We come to know not just what actions are right or wrong, but the essence of right and wrong itself. We become friends with right. We learn to recognize its character and presence. We love the presence of right; it lifts our souls and energizes us with vibrancy and vitality. Veering off the mark of God's design now feels heavy and lifeless. We recognize the restlessness and anxiety that lurks outside the realm of what is right. The distinction between what is and is not God's design grows more obvious, and we find ourselves rarely asking whether something is morally acceptable or not. This discernment guides us to be able to understand God's design for a host of areas. We discern God's design for relationships, parenting or running a business. Our lives build momentum as we live out of God's design in every area.

Humility

Our growth in obedience and integrity does not result in pride but rather humility. This is because we realize that none of this has been the fruit of our own labors. We did not make ourselves new; we did not have the ability to renew our own minds. We are not empowering our own obedience. Our journey is one of submission the entire way. We experience this as we get out of the way of God working within us. As a result, we are not impressed with ourselves but rather with the Lord. We recognize that the power belongs to the Lord and that He has shown just as much intentionality and ability toward every other element of creation as He has shown in our lives. We walk in awe of what the Lord has done in our own lives, and we look forward to seeing God move in that same way in the lives of people around us.

Generosity

The joy and freedom we experience from the Lord create in us a gratitude and a desire to give out of the fullness in which we now walk. We feel so given to, we want to give to others. We find ourselves desiring to give in every area. We give freely of our time and energy to the people who need it. We experience the joy of giving financially both to our local church and as God directs to other needs. We share truth and wisdom in the lives of others as we sense God's leading. In generosity, we experience the joy of participating in giving along with God. We do not give and find we have less than we started with, but we actually find we have more because we have given along with God.

Living on Mission with the Holy Spirit

As God continues to develop our connection with Him, growing us up more and more into Christ, He also welcomes us into a life of mission. We become vehicles of His transformation and rule in this world. We become partners with the Holy Spirit, looking to step in and cooperate with whatever He is presently doing. Our lives trend toward being people who are able to partner with whatever reality God's Kingdom is unleashing at present.

The foundation of the relationship and identity journeys God has taken us on prepares us for this missional lifestyle. We are rooted in God's love. Our needs for acceptance, security and belonging are met in the Lord, not fulfilled through the world. As a result, the enemy does not have the leverage to threaten to take these away from us. Additionally, we see and know who we are through God's truth about us. Our self-respect and sense of value come from our connection with the Lord's truth, not the opinions of others. All of this prepares us to approach our mission from a place of inner strength. We do not come to the world in need; our fundamental needs are met by God. As a result, we come to give life. We are able to give without needing something in return, and we are able to truly love the world around us.

Moving from the stable foundation of what God has built in our lives, we are able to take risks and join the Spirit in the adventure of releasing the Kingdom. This adventure becomes thrilling and wonderful instead of threatening or frightening (conditions that signal we are still looking for security or value). God has set us free to step into a lifestyle of partnership with the Spirit.

Mission

As we partner with God, we develop a sense of clear impact from our spiritual journey through the results of our partnership with the Kingdom. As this happens repeatedly, our lives take on a new sense of mission. We live with a sense of purpose as the reality of God's desire to actively partner with us becomes increasingly real. Our lives acquire new focus as our missions take precedence among the priorities in our lives. This happens naturally because the more we experience God's inbreaking activity, the more we find it fulfilling and satisfying. It truly is the calling we were meant for. There is a growing sense of purpose and significance to our lives.

Attention

We learn that when God is releasing His Kingdom, there is a window of opportunity to cooperate with Him. Furthermore, we recognize that our ability to discern the Spirit's leading has a lot to do with our own attentiveness to the present moment. Our attention becomes something we steward intentionally. We become aware that we shape our own experience of life according to what we choose to set our attention on. We take more and more control of our attention to prevent it from constantly being hijacked by the things of this world. In this, we shape our own experience of our minds, learning to keep ourselves in a place where we have enough mental room to stay connected to God and be alert to what He is doing.

Proactivity

Focusing our attention to recognize God's working trains us to take a proactive posture toward life. When God is moving, we do not want to miss out. We find ourselves taking bold chances because we do not want to let an opportunity pass. Beyond the direct partnership with God, we become people who default toward an active stance in life. We do not attempt to control. Rather, we believe we have input in our lives, and we use it to align with the Kingdom. We find ourselves leading, not always intentionally, but because we are more proactive than others who fall in line behind us. We experience God as we move forward and our faith becomes externally active.

Experiencing God

As we meet God through engaging in mission, we find ourselves experiencing Him more consistently than we previously believed was possible. Our lives truly feel like a partnership with God because He is active in it. We see Him show up in the lives of people around us, and we grow in experiencing His presence directly ourselves. We regularly have stories of experiencing God in one way or another. We find ourselves hungering more to experience His presence in our lives. As we seek His presence, our lives have a greater sense of His presence and guidance resting upon us. This partnership with God brings our relationship with Him to new places. God shares with us dimensions of relationship that are near to His heart. We find that He treats us as friends and partners or, even frighteningly at times, almost like peers.

Expectation

A growing sense of living with God and the ongoing experience of seeing God intersect people's lives develop an expectation of His activity. Instead of feeling like God *might* show up, we wait to see *how* God will show up. Faith stops feeling foreign to us as our experience of the Kingdom becomes consistently normal. The idea of problems existing without God in the equation feels strange; we fundamentally believe that God really does have the solution for and is involved in every situation. We find ourselves responding in ways that do not make sense from the outside. While some may have anxiety or concern, we have a genuine expectancy as we inwardly sense that natural problems do not hold a candle to the power of God.

Fellowship with the Spirit

Along the way, we get to know the Holy Spirit. Because we know Him so richly in our everyday lives, He stops feeling like the mysterious member of the Godhead. We know Him as God who is active all around us, and we grow acutely aware of how involved He is in our lives. We perceive Him actively dancing through situations, invisible to most people. We talk with Him and experience Him as a friend who shares our days. The work of the Kingdom becomes not just a noble cause we live toward but an ongoing opportunity to partner with our Best Friend.

Lifelong Growth

As we progress through our lives, God is always at work, developing us and growing us into the Gospel. We are constantly evolving in dynamic fellowship with the Father, Son and Spirit. Each layer builds upon the previous, drawing the course of our lives upward in increasing glory.

When we look at each of these stories sequentially, it might seem that once God develops the identity facet of the Gospel in our lives, we are done with relationship, and similarly when God moves on to the destiny component. In my experience, however, God is constantly bringing people through seasons that focus on each of these, constantly laying the foundation for the next portions of our journey. In the example of Maslow's pyramid, for the pyramid to get taller, every level needs to grow wider. Similarly, God works on alternate layers of the Gospel in our lives to develop us into everything He has for us.

I have found that as I journey, it is helpful to tune in to the layer in my life that God is working on at any given time. Each layer has a different character, and God works differently with each of them. As the practices we focus on shift, we focus more intentionally on connecting with a different member of the Godhead.

For example, until recently, the Father had me in a season of development in the relationship story. For a few months, I focused more heavily on worship and knowing God as the Father. I spent time getting in touch with His supremacy over creation and in seeing myself as His child. Just recently, I have felt a shift toward a season focused more on the identity story. I have been partnering with God to see myself more through His eyes in the specific way I am uniquely designed. I have been sinking my teeth into some areas of Scripture with a new depth, getting in touch with God's design in a deeper way in the areas of parenting and leadership.

If we intentionally partner with what God is doing, we can accelerate through each season more quickly and grow in it more deeply. I do not know about you, but I want my life to have a Kingdom impact, and that means I want to cover as much ground as I can. As we see what God is doing and yield to His transformational process, we become world changers.

Now that we have laid the groundwork of seeing the process of triune transformation personally, let us examine what it looks like to engage our communities in triune transformation as the Church.

IMPACT POINTS

- The process of triune transformation unleashes us into the fullest expression of our humanity.
- The Father's love sets us free from performance and makes us at home in His love.

- Being made new in Jesus the Son gives us an anchor point for our self-concept. We are freed to be who He says we are.

- With our needs for belonging and value met, we are free to pursue the Kingdom mission in connection with the Holy Spirit.

REBUILDING OUR COMMUNITIES

LEGOS WERE MY FAVORITE TOY growing up. I cannot tell you how many thousands of hours I spent poring over piles of pieces, searching for the right one to add to the creation I was building. Some of my best friendships were made around the LEGO pile as year by year we imagined and constructed. My friend James, who I have known since I was about two years old, had (and I think still has) the most enviable collection in the world. LEGOs helped my brother and me retain our sanity when we lived a year in China as the only English-speaking boys in the city of Hefei. I still have the set I purchased in Hong Kong during our Christmas break. I pull it out every few years and put it together. It is now my pleasure to introduce this same joy to my children, adding their collections to the one my parents saved from my childhood.

The creativity that LEGOs stimulate is beautiful: The countless hours of envisioning and creating left an indelible impression on my outlook on life. What makes LEGOs so brilliant is their systemic design. Every brick, block, pole, bridge and figure click together seamlessly. Everything connects to everything else, resulting in innumerable possibilities for construction. If you can dream it, you can build it. Brick by brick, you can build a fortress or a forest, a car or a castle, a submarine or a spaceship.

Just as LEGO blocks combine to form grander scenes, our lives are woven together with other lives in a seamless relational fabric we call society. None of us exists independently. We intersect with people at home, work and school. Our lives are our own, and yet no one is fully separate from others.

In this chapter, we will explore how the Gospel extends into the fabric of society. We have seen that the Gospel of the Kingdom is meant to redeem and transform both personal lives and society as a whole. Generally, however, the Church has been at a loss as to how to engage with society in a strategic and purposeful way. At times, we have had nothing more to offer than the advice to "Do good." As a result, many churches have outreaches but do not transform their communities.

There is a world of difference between engaging with your community and transforming your community. Jesus calls us to the latter. We as the Church have everything we need to change our communities if we will make room for God's Kingdom to come. Remember, *we* do not have the job of changing society. Our job is to let Jesus be King and let Him change society. That will happen if we cooperate with God's transformation process.

As we will see as we proceed through this chapter, when thinking about society, an awareness of the societal *level* at which we are working is critical for our effectiveness. The level that is immediately accessible and relevant to the local church is the starting place to practice our societal mission. To that end, let us look at God's calling to the Church in our communities.

Called to Rebuild Cities

For the last five hundred years of evangelical Christianity—essentially since the Reformation—much of the focus has been on individual salvation and our personal relationship with God.

Of course, I am all for this. I believe personal salvation is the non-negotiable starting point for the redemptive work of the Gospel in our lives. In this book so far, much of our attention has been on understanding and ministering the Kingdom on a personal scale, bringing healing to the sick, deliverance to the oppressed and so forth. And yet there is more.

The Scriptures often tie personal salvation with the idea of transforming society. Isaiah, for example, shares God's heart for His people in bringing redemption to the suffering and broken masses.

> Is not this the fast that I choose: to loose the bonds of wickedness, to undo the straps of the yoke, to let the oppressed go free, and to break every yoke? Is it not to share your bread with the hungry and bring the homeless poor into your house; when you see the naked, to cover him, and not to hide yourself from your own flesh? Then shall your light break forth like the dawn, and your healing shall spring up speedily; your righteousness shall go before you; the glory of the LORD shall be your rear guard.
>
> Isaiah 58:6–8

This is exactly what we have been talking about. As the chapter continues, the prophecy grows grander in scale.

> And your ancient ruins shall be rebuilt; you shall raise up the foundations of many generations; you shall be called the repairer of the breach, the restorer of streets to dwell in.
>
> Isaiah 58:12

Yes, God's desire is to use His people to rebuild individual lives, but it is also to restore the health of entire communities. This is part of the promises to the Church, the restored Israel (see Amos 9:14). Scripture even informs us that as he left his homeland, Abraham was pursuing a city from God (see Hebrews 11:10).

God wants to use us to release the city of His design and construction into our cities and communities. By and large, this is something the Church is not effective at, at least not in the West. Much of the time, the Church does not have a central role in the discussions that shape our communities or our nation. The groups that are driving the cultural discussions certainly are not the Church.

The stunning aspect of this is that, in some places, this is happening in the midst of an overwhelming majority of Christian believers. In the United States, as of this writing, the estimated percentage of followers of Jesus is close to seventy percent. How is it possible, then, that seven out of ten people in this country have some form of Christian faith, and yet the Church rarely has a place at the table of influence in our land?

I believe part of the issue is that we have bought into a fallacy of how society works. One of the primary strategies of evangelicalism in the last century has been to assume that if we could just get enough Christians at the baseline of society, the Christian influence would naturally drive its way up the ladder. If we get enough people saved and going to our churches, surely our culture will listen to us. At face value it sounds like a foolproof strategy.

The problem is that it has not worked. In fact, we have built some of the world's most significant Christian institutions in the last few decades, but our influence in broader culture continues to diminish. We have megachurches, but our communities are not being discipled by them. For the most part, society does not seem to care much at all. Building bigger churches or making more disciples is not enough to intrinsically bring healing to our communities.

We have been giving this subject a lot of thought in our church lately because we want to be a church that impacts our community. We want our community to love our church and be better for our presence. We want a place in the discussions shaping our community, and we want the opportunity to release the Kingdom to individuals, businesses, schools, civic government and beyond. In this chapter, we are going to explore some fruitful ideas for achieving these goals.

A Lesson from Science

To explain the reasoning here, I want to consider an interesting question that comes up in the study of physics. As budding physicists proceed through their training, they are eventually introduced to the wonderful and mysterious world of quantum mechanics—the physical laws governing atoms (atomic) and things smaller than atoms (subatomic). The quantum world of atoms and their subatomic pieces is about as bizarre and fantastic as you can imagine. Things teleport through time and space, particles randomly appear out of thin air and disappear just as quickly, and electrons in outer space can be made to rotate by rotating linked electrons on earth.

The further we peer into this marvelous science, the more we realize the world of the infinitesimally small works radically differently from our everyday world. Neils Bohr, one of the fathers of quantum theory, famously quipped, "Anyone who is not shocked by quantum theory has not understood it."

The typical reaction to quantum mechanics usually goes like this: *Hold on! How can the fundamental laws of quantum mechanics violate every natural law I know? Why doesn't the world I'm used to look at all like the subatomic world?*

These are fantastic questions. If quantum mechanics really is the foundation of nature, why does my everyday life not look like the quantum world? Why is my car not appearing and disappearing at will? Why does time not flow backward and forward?

Why, if my dog chases her tail, does a similar dog in Russia not instantly spin the exact same way?

It turns out that the way a system's elements organize themselves introduces new rules that apply to that level. For example, the rules of quantum mechanics describe how the individual atoms of hydrogen and oxygen behave, but in the common H_2O water molecule, where those atoms are bonded, the way the water molecules behave is governed by other rules that apply to molecules but not necessarily to individual atoms.

Scientists explain it this way: "The organization of the constituent atoms introduces rules of behavior, and those rules are not quantum mechanical." In lay terms: "The rules change when you take a step backward." The way things organize affects their behavior.

Now let us apply this to the world we live in, that of human beings. At the subatomic level (or scale), people are made up of individual atoms, which follow the rules of quantum mechanics. But it does not stop there. Follow this progression:

- The atoms arrange themselves into molecules, which follow the rules of molecular chemistry.
- The molecules arrange themselves into solids and liquids, which follow the rules of material science (solids) and fluid mechanics (liquids).
- The solids and liquids arrange themselves into cells, which follow rules of cellular biology.
- The cells arrange themselves into organs (heart, liver, lungs), which follow the rules of medical science.
- The organs arrange themselves into bodies and follow the rules of human beings.

Each layer of structure has its own description and rules that apply at that level.

The key thing for the Church to realize is that this same line of reasoning applies to individuals and their organizations. In the past, we have made the mistake of thinking that because we can influence individuals, we can change society. Yes, we have been tremendously effective at reaching people in their personal journeys, but we miss the fact that the way those individuals organize themselves creates additional rules that apply to the organizations (also called "systems"). These rules can negate the effects of individual change, thereby frustrating efforts to change the systems. Just like atoms, individual people organize themselves into systems (families, communities, societies) that follow different rules than do mere individuals. Changing the people in a system does not ensure a change in the system.

Consider a common example. When a believer with a dedicated walk of faith becomes romantically involved with an unbeliever, this often results in the believer being pulled away from his or her faith. Why does this happen? Well, the believer has become enmeshed in a structure that is exerting negative forces on him or her. This is the reason Paul tells us, "Do not be unequally yoked with unbelievers" (2 Corinthians 6:14). He understands that being tied together at different levels creates a structure that can undermine our faith journey.

Another example: Have you ever noticed how people change when they get around their families? Many a marriage has experienced tension over a spouse reverting to a previous version of himself or herself at the family reunion. Similarly, I often pray with college students who have discovered Jesus during their time in college and are concerned about returning home and staying true to their faith in that environment. Being organized into a family exerts a force on individuals because the rules of family are not the rules of individuals.

A useful analogy is the concept of leverage. Organizing in any form creates a situation where the structure has powerful leverage on the individuals within it.

Visuals are often very helpful when we are thinking about systems. Consider this diagram of an individual (the white box) in a relational system—perhaps this is the person's workplace:

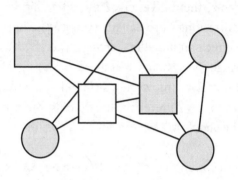

The circles and squares are individuals and the lines between the people represent the relationships between them. Just looking at this diagram, you can see this individual is going to be highly influenced by the system. If that square tries to move relative to the system, he or she is going to have to work against the force of four relationships. In fact, pushing or pulling on those relationships will move those individuals, which will then push or pull on their own collections of relationships. It is impossible for one part of the system to be affected without the whole system changing.

While this visual example may seem simplistic, it actually captures the dynamics well. This is the problem we face. It is not realistic to change individuals in the system and expect those changes to transform the system itself. Consider further the fact that society is made up of many subsystems: families make neighborhoods, neighborhoods make communities, communities make nations and so on. This is why we have not been particularly effective in our approach to changing the world.

If we want to see the Kingdom transform our cities and nations, we need to learn how the Gospel transforms not just individuals but systems. How does the Gospel apply to families, neighborhoods, schools and businesses?

We have been frustrated in our approach because we are trying to work in situations where we have minimal leverage. Rather than applying the Gospel to only the individuals in the system, we should also apply the Gospel to the *system itself*. If we are able to do that, we will see that the leverage indeed works the other way. The Gospel permeating the social system exerts leverage on the individuals within.

Connecting back to our discussion of society in chapter 4, we found there that Ephesus is an example of Paul reaching societal-level impact. Let us look at that a little closer. When the riot forms and the conflict begins, the silversmith Demetrius specifically argues that "the great goddess Artemis may be counted as nothing, and that she may even be deposed from her magnificence, she whom all Asia and the world worship" (Acts 19:27). Notice this detail: Artemis is worshiped in *all Asia*.

Earlier in the passage, we see the reason Artemis' power base is starting to crumble. After a brief period in the synagogue, Paul sets up shop in a school and forms a discipleship and mission center.

And he entered the synagogue and for three months spoke boldly, reasoning and persuading them about the kingdom of God. But when some became stubborn and continued in unbelief, speaking evil of the Way before the congregation, he withdrew from them and took the disciples with him, reasoning daily in the hall of Tyrannus. This continued for two years, so that all the residents of Asia heard the word of the Lord, both Jews and Greeks.

Acts 19:8–10

Paul's enterprise is so effective, it reaches all of Asia. This is why Artemis is beginning to be deposed. Paul has created a structure that mirrors the scale of her power base. Paul is working with the relational system of all of Asia and permeating it with the power of the Kingdom.

If we want to see the gods of the world overthrown and society discipled in the ways of Jesus, we must learn to do as Paul did and disciple social systems themselves.

The Church and Social Systems

As we saw earlier, the Church is the new nation that God is using to reach society. We know the Church is key to God's plan of redemption in this arena. Notice something interesting, though. The New Testament describes the Church as existing at *every* level in society. The society that is filled with believers in Jesus exists from a few individuals all the way up to the Church universal.

> For where two or three are gathered in my name, there am I among them.
>
> Matthew 18:20

> And day by day, attending the temple together and breaking bread in their homes, they received their food with glad and generous hearts.
>
> Acts 2:46

> To the angel of the church in Ephesus write: "The words of him who holds the seven stars in his right hand, who walks among the seven golden lampstands."
>
> Revelation 2:1

And he put all things under his feet and gave him as head over all things to the church, which is his body, the fullness of him who fills all in all.

Ephesians 1:22–23

The Church exists at various levels: a few gathered believers, a household group, a temple congregation, a city assembly and the Church universal. All of these are described as the Church because what makes the Church unique is the dynamics that govern social structures when groups of believers are gathered. It is what happens when God lives not only *within* people but *among* people, filling the social system that encompasses them. The Church is described as the system that exists between and around the people within it. "For just as the body is one and has many members, and all the members of the body, though many, are one body, so it is with Christ. . . . Now you are the body of Christ and individually members of it" (1 Corinthians 12:12, 27).

Whenever believers gather, they create the dynamic of the Church—the new-creation community. Why does this matter? It matters because whatever societal system we want to reach, there is a corresponding expression of the Church that exists at the same level. God has created a Church community that can exist at every level, from a few people gathered to the entire world united. He did this because there are worldly systems that need redemption at every scale. There is, therefore, no social institution to which the Church cannot apply appropriate leverage at a corresponding scale. This is how we work with the system as a whole, not just on the elements within the system.

Let us put some teeth on this and try to be more specific. What structures do we need to disciple and reach our communities?

Each person is slightly different, but most people have three spheres in which they live: home/family, vocation[1] and church. There are others with more spheres, but let us keep it simple.

193

Assume this is what it looks like.

If we think about it, each of these spheres has layers of organization that are embedded in a community. In the home sphere, people are organized into families, and families are organized into neighborhoods. Vocationally, people are often organized into teams or classrooms, and those are organized into businesses, schools, non-profits and so forth. In the church sector, depending on the size of the church, people are often organized into Bible classes, small groups and ministries that belong to the local church. It is the combination of the neighborhoods, vocational organizations and churches that make up the community.

In general, communities are made up of systems of different types of organizations. Organizations are systems of teams, and teams are systems of individuals. Each of these is replicated in these three sectors of home, vocation and church:

Name			System Structure	Size
Individual			Single	1
Family	Team	Small Group	System of Individuals	2–25
Neighborhood	Organization	Local Church	System of Teams	100–1,000
Community			System of Organizations	25,000+

When we lay it out this way, we see how the Church's present strategy yields the results we get and not the results we desire. We develop layers of church organization but we rarely task those layers with a mission beyond reaching individuals. We are not using leverage to adjust families, teams, neighborhoods or organizations. Instead, we are focused on changing individuals and hoping they will change the systems in which they are embedded. No wonder we are not seeing a lot of change three layers up in the community.

What would it look like to take a different approach and mobilize our layers of Church to engage their counterparts in the community? What if a small group of believers was trained in business to partner with, and minister to, community businesses? The group could take turns working with every business represented in the group. What would it look like for a church to build a partnership with a neighborhood? Rather than take up an offering to build an extension to their own building complex, the church could raise money for a new community center and staff it with volunteers.

If we want to create effective change in our communities, this kind of thinking gives us much greater leverage to make that happen.

The Triune Gospel Methodology

So, if we want to mobilize the Church in new ways, how do we do it? How do we aim toward our mission of releasing God's Kingdom into our communities at societal layers? Activity is not our goal; releasing the Kingdom is our goal. How does that work?

Historically, part of the breakdown has been our framing of the Gospel strongly from an individual point of view. It is not at all clear how that approach applies in the broader contexts of societal systems. We know individuals have sinned and need redemption, but how does that translate to ministering to our communities? Under the present paradigm, the only clear cause through which to engage communities is evangelism—saving the lost sinners—which we have done. But as we see, evangelism alone is not enough.

The Triune Gospel gives us some handles for how to think deeper about how the Gospel may work out in systemic constructs. Let us look at the pattern of transformation we saw in chapter 9 and understand how that works in a community. The transformational pattern of relationship, identity and destiny can be implemented in our communities when we make this key connection: The same pattern of relationship, identity and destiny persists both in individual and communal transformation. Jesus does it personally with us individually, and we as the Church do it with our communities. It is the same pattern. The pattern transcends the scale at which we are working. Because we may not have thought much about societal redemption, this might seem odd, but I am simply suggesting that we take the term "Body of Christ," which is all over the New Testament, and realize it is a literal description.

Relationship

The Church as an organization has a duty to organizational evangelism.

The first step is for an organization to come into relationship with God. How does that work? By coming into relationship with the *Church*. God has taken up residence in the Church in a unique way. We are His chosen, special possession. To connect with the Church is to connect with the God-liberated and God-empowered community. God indwells us as a system, and when that system is put in relationship with a less-godly system, that system comes into greater relationship with God.

Unfortunately, the Church has not done a great job with this because of our independent approach toward relationship with our communities. We have built walls instead of bridges, all the while praying for God to move in our communities. It is an approach that the Church is now reaping the fruit of as we fade into cultural irrelevance.

What if we treated our communities the way we treat unbelievers? We do not expect unbelievers to act like Christians. They are not, so why should they behave as we do? We love them despite the obvious need for God in their lives. We build relationship because we believe God loves everyone, believers and unbelievers, and in the context of relationship, we hope for the chance to share the Gospel. Unfortunately, we have done exactly the opposite in our communities.

We have built walls against hospitals because they perform abortions. Instead, we could build relationships around our joint value for healing. We have condemned our local governments because of corruption rather than connecting through our passion to see our communities be safe and productive. What if we stopped expecting these other organizations to act like the Church and just built relationship with them anyway? Does that sound like something Jesus might do? We might do well to focus less on pointing our fingers and more on washing their feet.

Identity

The next step is about identity, organizationally coming into alignment with a God-given design. God has created and appointed every industry. Government belongs to the King of Kings. Healthcare belongs to the Lord our Healer. Nutrition and fitness are about the body we have from the God in whom we live and move and have our being. Foodservice belongs to the Messiah, who prepared the Last Supper and looks forward to our next banquet. Education flows best from the one great Teacher, and entertainment echoes the stories and parables Jesus Himself spoke to the masses.

Each industry was dreamed in God's heart long before it ever was birthed on the earth. These industries have purpose and a design apart from the Church, and God values them. While our independent minds might believe that the ultimate redeemed community would have the Church as the only organization, I do not think this is God's goal at all. The completeness of what God has created in this world requires every industry to come into full expression. Remember, Israel had only one in twelve tribes that was dedicated by God to the tabernacle and priestly duties. That meant the other eleven had "secular" vocations designed and valued by God.

As the community from eternity, we can discern the ways of God for each vocation. We have access to the Lord, who designed every industry. As we build relationships and serve our communities, the Lord will give us opportunities to bring them into the fullness of their God-given design. Most industries could learn a lot from the Church. We capture people's hearts, while asking them to give us money, more effectively than most industries that pay their people for their allegiance. We teach people to serve better as volunteers than workers do on the clock. We help people become whole human beings, and every industry benefits from that. We also have people already embedded in many of these industries, people God wants to use powerfully within those contexts. On top of that, we have the Holy Spirit, who holds the keys for every industry.

Destiny

Finally, we should look at destiny and the Kingdom, stepping into God's mission organizationally. Drawing a parallel to how the Holy Spirit comes alongside believers and empowers us for mission, I am proposing joint missions between the Church and community organizations. We would find places of common mission and do good things for our community.

One reason the Church has not done well in this regard is our requirement of full alignment with our beliefs and values before we consider partnership with outside organizations. Remarkably, I do not see Jesus insisting on the same requirements. Even Judas got to jump in and demonstrate the Kingdom during Jesus' time on earth. Look at how Jesus handles it when another group, one that is not a part of the immediate community, is pursuing something that belongs to the Kingdom.

> John said to him, "Teacher, we saw someone casting out demons in your name, and we tried to stop him, because he was not following us." But Jesus said, "Do not stop him, for no one who does a mighty work in my name will be able soon afterward to speak evil of me. For the one who is not against us is for us."
>
> Mark 9:38–40

What if we went to our community centers in our less fortunate neighborhoods and offered to do a class on parenting? Surely it is not only Christians who want to learn how to raise children well. What if we asked the community if there were any old park district buildings we could refurbish and refresh? What if we gathered a bunch of substitute teachers and went to our local schools and told them we would like to give their teachers a day off a month at no cost? What if we found a local entrepreneurial group and offered them the use of our facilities for seminars? Even better, we could offer a speaker or two from members of our local church community.

These approaches can be neatly summarized with the New Testament's keywords for each of these stories: grace, righteousness and Kingdom of God. Our communities will be transformed as the Church learns to relate to organizations through grace instead of holding them captive to their sins. They will change as we learn to help them come into God's righteous design for their organization and partner with them to release God's Kingdom change into our communities.

This means working directly in the community system. We will be engaging the building blocks of cities, counties and neighborhoods instead of only the individuals populating these organizations. In fact, we will see that working with the system will get individual members moving into the things of the Kingdom much quicker. As we partner to work within the community system directly, we will see the system of the whole community released into things of God.

One last thought: This whole process will be significantly accelerated if we pursue it in conjunction with other churches in our community. This interdependent relationship increases Kingdom leverage all the more.

God wants to bring redemption to our communities. Remember, the final image in the Bible is a holy city, the new Jerusalem, coming down from heaven to earth. God's heart is to renew our communities . . . through the Church.

These Ideas in Action

We are still really exploring this kind of thinking and activity in our church, but the early fruit has been so exciting that I just have to share it. It really changes everything to have your church engaged with releasing life to your local community. Up until now, I have attempted to sketch a general framework that should be applicable in any context. To flesh it out more fully, I would like to close this chapter with two illustrations.

Story One

A few years ago, the pastor of one of the churches that has been a partner of ours for years was looking at upcoming events on his city's website. He noticed a family festival and called up the city to ask if they needed any help and if his church could serve the city at the event.

The city was thrilled the church actually wanted to help, and they asked the church to run their booths at the festival. The church staffed every booth and added one of their own as a place for people to get prayer if they were interested. The church volunteers all wore shirts that read, "How can I pray for you?" People were talking and praying throughout the event.

After the event, the mayor thanked the church, saying it was the smoothest event the city had ever run and that it was all because of the church's help. Afterward, the park director offered the city's facilities to the church anytime for church events or outreaches.

The church has continued to serve the community, serving concessions and helping park cars during city movie nights. In time, the city asked if they could move the city movie night to the church property, since the church parking lot held more cars than the city park. The city further requested their help at Halloween and Easter events, and the pastors have decided to lay down their own outreaches to commit themselves to serving the city.

At each turn, they have been requested not only to help but also to "make sure you wear those 'Pray For You?' shirts." The city is asking them to pray at their city events! This past Easter, the city asked for the church to set up a table to promote their Easter services at the city event. It is so exciting to see the local city government resourcing the church to be the church in their community.

Story Two

The church I pastor is a multisite church, and one of our campuses has about five hundred attendees in a town of about five thousand. We have been experimenting there, knowing we have a lot of leverage in that community. Last year, that campus purchased a building in their community that formerly housed a big-box store. After we purchased the building, we had the value reassessed. We then decided to leave it on the tax roll even though we could have removed it. We realized that for us to take the taxes off the building would be to remove income from the community, and we did not want to do that, especially since the community had been struggling with a high poverty rate.

When we told the local government officials we planned to pay taxes on the building, they were shocked. They had not expected us to be thinking of their benefit along with ours. As a result, the leaders began to join us at roundtable discussions about the future of the community. They saw we were truly there for the benefit of the community, and so they wanted to join us at the table. Our campus pastor began to ask how we could use the building in a way that truly benefited the community.

A few weeks after the first meeting, a check made out for $10,000 arrived in the mail. The campus pastor was amazed. This was more than the annual taxes on the new building. A week or so after that, a local business leader asked for a phone call. When the campus pastor connected with him, the business leader said he liked the direction things were headed and wanted to partner with us. He had written that check and said that because he believed in what we were doing, he was going to invest in the city through us at $10,000 a month for at least the rest of the year. Someone who does not even attend our church was giving to the building and beyond.

While we set about figuring out exactly what to do with the building and the gift, an elderly couple came to us and said they liked what we were doing in the community. This couple was in their seventies and had run a daycare for years. The daycare had about one hundred kids, was fully staffed, had a paid-off building and a little less than $200,000 in the bank. The couple had run it their whole lives and did not want to see their life's work pass away. They asked us if we would be willing to take the whole thing, free of charge, on the condition that we would keep it running as a daycare. The children's pastor, who has a master's in education, just about did cartwheels down the hallway.

So now we are getting paid by parents to pour into the next generation of kids and train them in the things of the Kingdom while a local business is paying for a building and ministry that will benefit the whole community.

Sound unbelievable? This is what God's Kingdom looks like as it works its way through a community. God's reign works by a different set of rules than the world's rules. This is what it looks like when new-creation societal dynamics kick in.

I believe our communities are waiting for the Church to step fully into her role as the community of the new creation. Until then, communities remain caught in the bondage of the powers of this world—powers that the Church has the ability to dislodge. We have been given what we need to partner with God to release life in our communities and see the Kingdom reshape them after God's design. Jesus has purchased a whole new world, and we get to be on the front seat of seeing Him release it in the communities where we live.

IMPACT POINTS

- If we want to see any system (including cities or nations) transformed, we need to make sure we are working at a level that is appropriate to change the system.
- The Church exists at every layer of organization there is, and as such, it has the ability to work redemptively in any social context.
- The Triune Gospel provides a way forward in our communities when we see that the Church is the organizational presence of God in our cities and communities.

12

LOOKING TO THE HORIZON

SQUINTING THEIR EYES in the midday heat, the eleven re-maining disciples followed Jesus on a dusty path that led up the side of the mountain. The last forty days had been such a whirl-wind. First recovering from the shock of seeing their Teacher alive again, then trying to wrestle through what it meant, all the while Jesus was appearing and vanishing into thin air as He shared with them about the new world He was starting.

In typical form, Jesus had not revealed where they were going on this excursion or why they were headed there. He had simply come to them that morning with the ever-present twinkle in His eyes and said, "Hey guys, follow Me." The disciples had long ago stopped trying to figure Jesus out and realized that obedience was far more important than understanding.

Even though they had not yet been in Jerusalem even two months, this mountain was already replete with memories. That first week, Jesus had taught in the temple every day, but after-ward, He and the disciples would retreat to the mountain to de-brief and lodge for the evenings.

The disciples chatted with each other as they went.

"What is it with Jesus and mountains, anyway?"

"He loves them, doesn't He?"

"Hey, James. Is this what it was like that time He started *glowing?*"

"Sort of, I guess. I mean, that mountain was a lot taller."

"Man, I wish He would have brought *me* along."

They rounded a bend and fell silent as the garden by the city came into view. That was where everything began the tumble downward. They had slept as Jesus prayed, and then Judas, that traitor, had come with the soldiers. Even with the proof that Jesus had emerged victorious—was He not leading them at this very moment?—the disciples still were not ready to face their own regrets.

Their Master turned back, a grin on His face. "Come on, guys, just a little farther."

"Hey, I think I know where He's taking us," Thomas said. He was always good at connecting the dots and jumping to where things were headed. "It's that place where He told us about the unraveling of this age."

"All that stuff about war and death and slaughter?"

"Yikes, that still gives me chills."

"Why would Jesus take us back there?"

Sure enough, a little farther up, Jesus stopped near some familiar rock slabs. The disciples sat down, wondering what exactly Jesus meant by bringing them back to the place of such a foreboding discussion.

"Guys, it's really important that you stay here in Jerusalem," He said.

The disciples shot glances among themselves. Was this a farewell speech? Surely not. Why would Jesus go through all of that and then leave?

"This whole thing starts in Jerusalem, guys, so you gotta stay here. Jerusalem was the capital of the old Israel, and this is where God wants to fulfill His promise. Remember when my cousin John promised that I would baptize with the Holy Spirit?"

Old Israel . . . the promise of the new covenant and the Spirit. The disciples knew God had promised to restore the glory of Israel at the end of all things. The disciples sat in silence, their minds struggling to put it all together.

Then, in a flash of insight, one of them saw it. Israel was doomed to die; this is what Jesus had told them. But Jesus, the King of the Jews, had already died—only now Jesus was alive again.

"Wait . . . Lord . . . are you restoring the Kingdom to Israel *right here? Right now?* Are *we* Israel resurrected? Are we going to be filled with the power of Your resurrection to fulfill our destiny to the nations?"

A smile broke across Jesus' face. The Spirit within them was already putting the picture together. This was going to be fun to watch.

"Don't worry about the timing. The Father will take care of that. Here is what you need to know: The Holy Spirit is the power source. When He comes upon you, the same way you've seen Him upon me, you'll have what you need. Proclaim that I'm King of the new Israel. Start here in Jerusalem, and this new Israel will spread throughout the twelve tribes and to the ends of the earth."

The disciples were reeling as they mouthed, "Ends of the earth? Us?"

"It's okay." Jesus continued. "All authority in the heavens and over all the nations has been given to Me. You do not go on your own authority. You go in my name." Jesus raised His hands over them. "I bless you now to go and make disciples of all the nations. You will baptize them into the name of the Father and the Son and the Holy Spirit. You will guide them into My ways. You have what you need. I will be with you always, even to the end of the age."

With that, Jesus rose into the sky. Awestruck, the disciples watched Him as the clouds carried Him upward and out of sight. They stood there for a long time, looking into the sky and wondering if they would ever see Him again. Then a voice behind them spoke.

"Hey . . . guys?"

Shocked, they whirled around to see two people clad in white who were definitely not there a few minutes ago.

"Hey, don't you have instructions to follow? In due time, Jesus will return the same way you just saw Him leave. Why don't you guys head back to Jerusalem like He told you."

The eleven made their way back down the mountain, realizing the world would never be the same. They had come up the mountain seeing themselves as eleven disciples. They were descending knowing they were new Israel, a nation born again of the resurrection and soon to be filled with the power to bring life to every person and nation.

Ten days later, the promised Holy Spirit would be poured out. The power of the life from eternity would come upon them and empower them to overthrow the works of the enemy. The nations would be gathered back together as the Spirit bridged the language gap that had driven them apart thousands of years earlier. The rule of God, through the new Israel, was now headed to the ends of the earth.

The Journey Here and the Journey Ahead

Nearly twenty centuries later, you and I are part of that same new Israel, sent with the same calling. There is no greater task imaginable than to baptize the world in the power of life that has come crashing into our lives. The torch has been passed, generation to generation, as God's Kingdom continues to invade the world and displace the power of the enemy.

We began our journey asking ourselves why our faith did not seem to make much difference in the world around us. Like the disciples in the previous story, it is possible that we have been following Jesus without understanding the cause to which He has invited us. This book has been a walk up a winding trail to see more clearly the mission of our faith. It has taken twists and turns, and quite possibly presented familiar sights from new vantage points. Ultimately, our desire has been to step into the very center of what Jesus is doing in this world. It is there that Jesus Himself is waiting to meet us.

This is where we have been.

We have seen that to follow Jesus is to follow a world changer. His version of faith leaves a footprint in the world around us, and our faith ought to do the same. The Kingdom of God He announces is all about God's intersection with the world to bring wholeness into brokenness.

We have seen that God's Kingdom is disrupting both personal and societal evil. Through Jesus' atoning sacrifice, He provides freedom from both of these. The task of our faith, therefore, is to proclaim and demonstrate Jesus' rule and partner with Him to bring every part of the world into alignment with His life from eternity.

We have discovered that the Holy Spirit is the one who unleashes the power of the coming age into this present time. As the Word and the Spirit come together, the new creation is released. The works of darkness are displaced, and God's rule is established.

We have peered into the mysteries of a Triune Gospel, one that mirrors God Himself. We have discovered the Gospel is three distinct stories: (1) coming back into relationship with the Father, (2) being made new in the Son and (3) releasing the Kingdom through the power of the Spirit. These three threads are woven into one glorious Gospel that God uses to transform us and bring us into the fullness of His design for our lives and society.

We have seen that the Church in our day is at a hinge point. Society is pivoting into a new era, and it is time for us to leave behind an independent posture so that we can once again assume the role of discipling the nations. We have discussed how the Triune Gospel provides the roadmap for us to work redemptively, not only in individual lives but in our communities as well.

This journey, of course, is merely the invitation to the real task. We have outlined how it works. What remains is to step fully into it. Like the disciples, we too could easily be staring into the sky when Jesus has called us to work. Now the true calling is at hand: to step in for ourselves; to connect with and be filled with the Holy Spirit, who is amazing at combating the personal and societal evil in the world; to roll up our sleeves and join the Spirit in His work to release the Kingdom in people's lives and in our communities. We have joined the fathers of our faith in understanding the task. Now let us join them in the field of harvest. We have talked about it—now is the time to descend the mountain and do it.

As I look to the future, I am so excited. We have already examined the power of churches united in peer-level interdependent relationships with their community. Imagine if those interdependent collections of churches began to form relationships with each other across our states and nations. What would it look like for churches to actually have enough relationship with each other that they could apply real Kingdom leverage to the problems of an entire state or country? For the first time in human history, that is realistically achievable given the wonders of modern technology and the connection it facilitates.

I mentioned that after encountering the Kingdom in China, we started a training school called the School of Kingdom Ministry. By planning from the beginning to form interdependent relationships with our hosting churches and leveraging technological connection, our little training school has rapidly grown throughout the United States and the world. We have equipped and trained thousands, and we have hundreds of friends in cities around the world who are working to raise up and mobilize believers for this Kingdom task. Most weeks I impact the world and never leave home.

If this is what happens when a little training class steps into God's Kingdom future, what can happen when an entire *local church* steps in? I believe this is the way the Lord is giving us to disciple the nations.

If our faith lacks purpose, it is because we have not joined Jesus' task, for indeed Jesus' call to us is the most profoundly significant undertaking there is. We are here to bridge His new creation with our world. I absolutely believe that with Him it is possible to do what He asks of us. Jesus has not given us the task knowing we cannot do it. He has filled us with His resurrection life, knowing it is the most powerful force in the universe.

Keeping our eyes fixed on the greatness of our God, let us now undertake this great task together.

NOTES

Chapter 2: Jesus' Message and Model

1. A point of clarity: In the other gospels, the language "Kingdom of God" is typically used, whereas Matthew uses the language "Kingdom of Heaven." These are not two distinct kingdoms. Rather, Matthew is writing primarily to a Jewish audience and, as such, is avoiding the divine name, Yahweh, as the Jews felt His name was too holy to be used in a typical setting. The two terms are synonymous.

2. *The New International Dictionary of New Testament Theology and Exegesis* puts it this way, "Its meaning is perhaps best captured by the English 'kingship,' though the nuance may be varied: the fact of being king, or the king's position/power/office, or his active rule, etc." Moisés Silva, *The New International Dictionary of New Testament Theology and Exegesis*, 2nd ed., vol. 1 (Grand Rapids: Zondervan, 2014), 474–475.

3. The language Jesus uses at times is that it is so close, it is "at hand"—within grasping distance. This is an apt metaphor because it describes God's initiation to bring His Kingdom close; it further describes our response necessary to receive that Kingdom into our lives.

4. Or, if you will: "The time is fulfilled, and the kingdom of God is at hand; repent and believe in the gospel" (Mark 1:15).

Chapter 3: Restoring Our Lives

1. This is what Jesus hints at when He tells His disciples to partake of Him and receive life (see John 6:53–54).

Chapter 4: Reclaiming the Planet

1. Google search for "facebook headquarters hacker way aerial view" if you would like to see it yourself.

2. If you would like to dig deeper into understanding the supernatural beings outlined in the Bible and how they fit in the story, check out Dr. Michael S. Heiser's fantastic book *The Unseen Realm*.

3. See Exodus 12:12, Psalm 82, Psalm 97:7, Psalm 138:1 and 1 Corinthians 8:5.

4. I should note that some translations use the term "sons of Israel" instead of "sons of God" in this verse, but logically that does not make sense because Israel is not a nation until well after this event. Jacob/Israel himself has not even been born yet. "Sons of God" is the clear translation, it is just that most translation committees do not have a supernatural paradigm and do not know what to do with the verse.

5. This last point of Jesus drawing all peoples to Himself is made more evident in the context of the passage, which comes after some Greeks come seeking Jesus (see John 12:20–22). Jesus then talks about His death, since that is the key to restoring the nations to Himself.

6. If you want to explore this line of reasoning further, dig into N. T. Wright's *The Day the Revolution Began.*

7. In chapter 9, we will discover why these three specific categories are especially significant.

8. All four gospels directly record the conversation that Jesus and Pilate have about Jesus' kingship as well as the inscription "King of the Jews" placed above Him on the cross. Anything that all four gospels record is something the Bible is highlighting and specifically drawing our attention to.

9. There are some people who make a practice of trying to engage with these god figures in spiritual battle, casting them down to liberate cities, and so forth. I am honestly not sure what I think about that. I know that in this book we will look at a different strategy that fits more in line with the concepts we are developing as we go.

Chapter 5: A World at War

1. In this viewpoint, not every event is directly good or evil. Many events may just be events that happen. Once again, it is important to distinguish between events that we *like* and events that are revealed to be *good*, as these are two different categories. We are discussing good and evil here.

2. This logic is a bit muddled and confuses the attribute of sovereignty with a given model for how that sovereignty works. In all of these viewpoints, we can assert that God is both good and sovereign. The relevant question at hand is how that goodness and sovereignty is defined. Proposing a different goodness/sovereignty model is far from properly labeled as heresy.

Chapter 6: The Spirit and Kingdom

1. I have never stood in line overnight to buy an Apple product, so do not judge me too harshly, but I do admit that I am typing on a Mac as I write this.

2. Verses 7–11 address the gifts of the Spirit, verses 12–27 address the services from the Lord and verses 28–31 address the activities empowered by God.

3. Brian blogs many of his God adventures on his website at kingdomencounters .com. Inspirational reading.

Chapter 7: Partnering with God Today

1. The verb tense on "be filled" is a present-tense verb used to indicate that being filled with the Spirit is not a once-for-all experience but a repeated empowering as the Spirit provides. My adjustment from the ESV is to make this present tense clearer. For more information, see the notes on Ephesians 5:18 in the *Zondervan NASB Study Bible* (Grand Rapids: Zondervan, 1999).

2. I tend to see this as *both*: a suggestion that comes from the enemy which is caught and magnified by our own desires until we reach the moment of choice.

Chapter 8: The Times They Are A-Changin'

1. I find it fascinating that these transitions even seem to be happening at about the same age that we as individuals experience them, when you count in centuries instead of years.

Chapter 9: The Triune Gospel

1. I am drawing the Triune Gospel in the same shape as the Trinity to draw a parallel between the two. I am not implying the Gospel is the Trinity but rather that the Trinity and the Gospel share the same structure.

2. Within Christianity there has been virtually endless debate as to how to understand the atonement. What I am proposing is that the atonement is multifaceted and that multiple understandings are accurate because the atonement works differently in each of these stories.

Chapter 11: Rebuilding Our Communities

1. I use the term *vocation* to denote the productive role someone serves in society, be it through work, receiving education, volunteering or so on.

In the process of obtaining a Ph.D. in theoretical quantum physics, **Putty Putman** ran headlong into the power and reality of the Holy Spirit during a supernatural encounter in China. Following the leading of Jesus to sell everything he had to purchase "the pearl of great price," Putty terminated a successful career in physics to pursue learning, leading and training others to move in the power of the Holy Spirit.

Putty is on the senior leadership team of the Vineyard Church of Central Illinois. He co-leads the preaching team, and he oversees the School of Kingdom Ministry—a supernatural training and discipleship school hosted by local churches across the country and around the world. A gifted communicator and passionate equipper, Putty loves to see people grow in the conviction of who they are in Christ and be released to live a naturally supernatural lifestyle empowered by the Holy Spirit.

Putty lives in Champaign, Illinois, with his wife, Brittany, and three children. For more information, see:

puttyputman.com
facebook.com/puttyputman
thevineyardchurch.us
schoolofkingdomministry.org

Be who God made you

school of KINGDOM MINISTRY

Join thousands of believers around the world on a journey of discovering who you are in Christ and being released to move in the power of the Holy Spirit. **The School of Kingdom Ministry** is hosted at local churches and partners with pastors and leaders to bring supernatural discipleship to your church, family and community.

Join the family and take the journey of discovering the life God has for us all!

SCHOOLOFKINGDOMMINISTRY.ORG

Also from Putty Putman

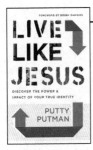

What if there is more to the Gospel than we imagined? What if a life of more lies not in what you do but in who you are? When you discover the power of your true identity, you will discover a vibrant, thrilling life of impact, adventure and freedom—a life, like Jesus', that is connected to and empowered by a God who is and does more than we ever imagined.

Live Like Jesus